Validity, Reliability, and Significance

Empirical Methods for NLP and Data Science

Synthesis Lectures on Human Language Technologies

Editor
Graeme Hirst, *University of Toronto*

Synthesis Lectures on Human Language Technologies is edited by Graeme Hirst of the University of Toronto. The series consists of 50- to 150-page monographs on topics relating to natural language processing, computational linguistics, information retrieval, and spoken language understanding. Emphasis is on important new techniques, on new applications, and on topics that combine two or more HLT subfields.

Syntax-based Statistical Machine Translation
Philip Williams, Rico Sennrich, Matt Post, and Philipp Koehn
2016

Domain-Sensitive Temporal Tagging
Jannik Strötgen and Michael Gertz
2016

Linked Lexical Knowledge Bases: Foundations and Applications
Iryna Gurevych, Judith Eckle-Kohler, and Michael Matuschek
2016

Bayesian Analysis in Natural Language Processing
Shay Cohen
2016

Metaphor: A Computational Perspective
Tony Veale, Ekaterina Shutova, and Beata Beigman Klebanov
2016

Grammatical Inference for Computational Linguistics
Jeffrey Heinz, Colin de la Higuera, and Menno van Zaanen
2015

Automatic Detection of Verbal Deception
Eileen Fitzpatrick, Joan Bachenko, and Tommaso Fornaciari
2015

Natural Language Processing for Social Media
Atefeh Farzindar and Diana Inkpen
2015

Semantic Similarity from Natural Language and Ontology Analysis
Sébastien Harispe, Sylvie Ranwez, Stefan Janaqi, and Jacky Montmain
2015

Learning to Rank for Information Retrieval and Natural Language Processing, Second Edition
Hang Li
2014

Ontology-Based Interpretation of Natural Language
Philipp Cimiano, Christina Unger, and John McCrae
2014

Validity, Reliability, and Significance: Empirical Methods for NLP and Data Science
Stefan Riezler and Michael Hagmann

ISBN: 978-3-031-01055-2 paperback
ISBN: 978-3-031-02183-1 ebook
ISBN: 978-3-031-00194-9 hardcover

DOI 10.1007/978-3-031-02183-1

A Publication in the Springer Nature series
SYNTHESIS LECTURES ON ADVANCES IN AUTOMOTIVE TECHNOLOGY

Lecture #55
Series Editor: Graeme Hirst, *University of Toronto*
Series ISSN
Print 1947-4040   Electronic 1947-4059

Validity, Reliability, and Significance

Empirical Methods for NLP and Data Science

Stefan Riezler

Department of Computational Linguistics
& Interdisciplinary Center for Scientific Computing
Heidelberg University, Heidelberg, Germany

Michael Hagmann

Department of Computational Linguistics
Heidelberg University, Heidelberg, Germany

SYNTHESIS LECTURES ON HUMAN LANGUAGE TECHNOLOGIES #55

ABSTRACT

Empirical methods are means to answering methodological questions of empirical sciences by statistical techniques. The methodological questions addressed in this book include the problems of validity, reliability, and significance. In the case of machine learning, these correspond to the questions of whether a model predicts what it purports to predict, whether a model's performance is consistent across replications, and whether a performance difference between two models is due to chance, respectively. The goal of this book is to answer these questions by concrete statistical tests that can be applied to assess validity, reliability, and significance of data annotation and machine learning prediction in the fields of NLP and data science.

Our focus is on model-based empirical methods where data annotations and model predictions are treated as training data for interpretable probabilistic models from the well-understood families of generalized additive models (GAMs) and linear mixed effects models (LMEMs). Based on the interpretable parameters of the trained GAMs or LMEMs, the book presents model-based statistical tests such as a validity test that allows detecting circular features that circumvent learning. Furthermore, the book discusses a reliability coefficient using variance decomposition based on random effect parameters of LMEMs. Last, a significance test based on the likelihood ratio of nested LMEMs trained on the performance scores of two machine learning models is shown to naturally allow the inclusion of variations in meta-parameter settings into hypothesis testing, and further facilitates a refined system comparison conditional on properties of input data.

This book can be used as an introduction to empirical methods for machine learning in general, with a special focus on applications in NLP and data science. The book is self-contained, with an appendix on the mathematical background on GAMs and LMEMs, and with an accompanying webpage including R code to replicate experiments presented in the book.

KEYWORDS

empirical methods, measurement theory, validity, bias features, circularity, generalized additive models, deviance, nullification, reliability, experimental design, variance components, linear mixed models, orthogonal estimators, significance, likelihood ratio

To Sabine and Janna & Ida.

Contents

Preface

There is a particular book that accompanied the first author since his days as doctoral student: Paul R. Cohen's textbook *Empirical Methods for Artificial Intelligence* [Cohen, 1995]. The book was introduced to him by Mark Johnson, with the recommendation that it contained essential information for an empirical researcher that is not easily available in a comparably concise form anywhere else. This assessment of Cohen's book is still valid today.

Myriad books on machine learning, deep learning, and artificial intelligence have been published since Cohen's book appeared in 1995. With rare exceptions such as Hardt and Recht [2021], however, questions about data practices, the concepts of validity and reliability, or techniques of exploratory data analysis are not mentioned in contemporary books on machine learning. A discussion of confirmatory techniques for statistical hypothesis testing and their relevance for practical machine learning research is also not integrated in most machine learning textbooks. For these topics, Cohen's exposition of exploratory and confirmatory techniques of empirical science is still the to-go textbook. However, Cohen's book has not been updated since its publication date.

The goal of our book is to extend and update Cohen's book using model-based techniques to address the questions of validity, reliability, and significance in empirical machine learning research. In our book, these techniques are based on interpretable probabilistic models as described in Wood [2017]. These models are not necessarily more recent than Cohen's book, but they possess the necessary expressiveness to model experimental data from data annotation and machine learning prediction experiments, and they are associated with proven statistical properties for drawing inferences about the parameters and models. The goal of our book is to provide the reader with an instrument in the form of model-based statistical tests that enables assessing the methodological questions of validity, reliability, and significance. We showcase our techniques on examples from the authors' areas of expertise—NLP and medical data science—and hope that the proposed techniques will also be of use to readers from other areas of machine learning and artificial intelligence.

Stefan Riezler and Michael Hagmann
November 2021

Acknowledgments

This book would not have been possible without the help of several people who are actively involved in empirical machine learning research, and who were willing to read early drafts of our book and comment on its relevance to their own work.

Firstly, we would like to thank the students at the departments of computational linguistics and computer science who participated in two iterations of a seminar class on the topics of the book, and who detected and corrected many mistakes in earlier versions of the book. We are indebted to Nathan Berger for proofreading our writing as a native speaker of American English and for comments on the intelligibility of the contents as a Ph.D. student in computer science. We would like to thank Michael Staniek for his critical comments on the coherence of our argumentation and the usefulness of the presented methods for a Ph.D. student in computational linguistics. We are indebted to Mayumi Ohta for testing our R scripts and for contributing to the experimental material that illustrates our statistical tests.

We thank Artem Sokolov for patiently going over several early versions of the book, for a great many discussions on all aspects of our work, and for serving as an endless source of recommendations on related work.

Last, we would like to thank Graeme Hirst and Michael Morgan for giving us the chance to publish this book in the first place and for selecting two excellent reviewers. We thank the anonymous reviewers for providing feedback on all levels of detail of the book and for giving invaluable guidance on how to present our material in a clear and appealing form.

Clearly, various errors and shortcomings remain, and we would be grateful if readers could point them out to us so that they can be corrected.

Stefan Riezler and Michael Hagmann
November 2021

CHAPTER 1

Introduction

1.1   EMPIRICAL METHODS IN MACHINE LEARNING

Machine learning is a research field that has been explored for several decades, and recently has begun to affect many areas of modern life under the reinvigorated label of artificial intelligence. The goal of machine learning can be described as learning a mathematical function to make predictions on unseen test data, based on given training data, without explicit programmed instructions on how to perform the task. The methods employed for learning functional relationships between inputs and outputs heavily build on methods of mathematical optimization [Bottou et al., 2018]. While optimization problems are formalized as minimization of empirical risk functions on given training data, the important twist in machine learning is that it aims to optimize prediction performance in expectation, thus enabling generalization to unseen test data. The development and analysis of techniques for generalization is the topic of the dedicated sub-field of statistical learning theory [Bousquet et al., 2004, Vapnik, 1998, von Luxburg and Schölkopf, 2011]. Statistical learning theory can be seen as the methodological basis of machine learning, and central concepts of statistical learning theory have been compared to Popper's ideas of falsifiability of a scientific theory [Corfield et al., 2009]. In a similar spirit, comparisons of the methodology of machine learning and empirical science have led to direct advertisements of "Machine Learning as Philosophy of Science" [Korb, 2004].

Let us contrast this proposition with the practical workflow of a machine learning researcher conducting empirical research in natural language processing (NLP) and data science. Most empirical research in these areas follows the paradigm of adopting or establishing a set of input representations and output labels that are split into portions for training, development, and testing. The data in these splits are assumed to represent independent samples from an identical distribution (so-called i.i.d. samples). Furthermore, data in the splits are made i.i.d. artificially, e.g., by shuffling data at random between splits [Arjovsky et al., 2019] or by experience replay [Schölkopf, 2019]. The i.i.d. assumption is crucial for the consistency guarantees from statistical learning theory to apply [Vapnik, 1998, von Luxburg and Schölkopf, 2011]. Furthermore, it can be seen an acknowledgment of basic principles of experimental control by a randomized experimental design [Cox and Reid, 2000, Mead et al., 2012]. A typical NLP or data science project then starts with optimizing the parameters of a machine learning model on given training data, tuning meta-parameters on development data, and ends with testing the model using a standard automatic evaluation metric on benchmark test data. We call this scheme of a machine learning process the **train-dev-test paradigm** of NLP and data science.[1]

The train-dev-test paradigm allows the researcher to happily focus on improving model performance, with the only limit being the computational budget to train and re-train complex models, such as deep neural networks, under extensive exploration of meta-parameters, but without having to ask any questions about the data themselves, about what the machine learning model learned from them, or how the learning process is influenced by diverse sources of variability. Such questions are typically thought of as extraneous to the machine learning process, and standard statistical learning theory does not provide answers to them. However, as we will show in this book, processes like data annotation or model evaluation that happen before or after machine learning crucially influence the entire machine learning process. The viewpoint advocated in this book is that answers to questions about bias and consistency in data annotation, about representations of raw input data, or about variability of machine learning models with respect to meta-parameters and test data, should be an integral part of the methodology of machine learning. The current discussion of methodological issues in empirical machine learning is at the state of informal guidance by Dos and Don'ts [Bowman and Dahl, 2021, Lones, 2021]. The goal of this book is to analyze problems in the train-dev-test paradigm from the viewpoint of the methodology of empirical sciences—a point of view that is independent of and orthogonal to statistical learning theory[2]—and to answer them by concrete statistical techniques.

The methodological questions that will be addressed in this book include the question of **validity**—does a machine learning model predict what it purports to predict? For example, we might want to scrutinize surprisingly good results on hard tasks like natural language understanding, and ask whether successful machine learning models do understand language or instead rely on superficial patterns that are highly, but spuriously, correlated with target classes [Clark et al., 2019]. Similarly, observed superior performance in data mining might be due to illegitimate leakage of information correlated with the target [Kaufmann et al., 2011], and exact prediction of the target in medical informatics might be based on using defining features of the target as input features to machine learning models in a circular way [Schamoni et al., 2019]. The second important question that we will address is that of **reliability**—how consistent is a performance evaluation if replicated for the same model trained under different meta-parameter settings? While approaches have been presented that report expected validation performance with respect to a computational budget instead of reporting only single best results [Dodge et al., 2019, Henderson et al., 2018, Lucic et al., 2018], it is furthermore important to analyze the contribution of different sources of variance to performance results, including model architec-

---

[1]Clearly, this paradigm is pervasive in machine learning and artificial intelligence in general, for example, in the area of image processing that uses similar methods and exhibits similar problems as the area of natural language processing. We will frequently refer to examples from related areas, but keep our focus on running examples from the areas of NLP and medical data science.

[2]The orthogonality of our methodological point of view to statistical learning theory is shown by the fact that it applies to classical learning theory as well as to more recent approaches [Arjovsky et al., 2019, Kawaguchi et al., 2020, Shen et al., 2021].

tures, meta-parameters, and the benchmark data themselves, in order to make reported results interpretable and replicable. Last, we will discuss the question of **significance**—how likely is it that an observed difference between evaluation results of two models is due to chance? The current state-of-the-art consists of matching performance evaluation metrics to statistical significance tests, and devising specialized techniques for testing hypotheses across multiple solutions and multiple test sets [Dror et al., 2020]. However, there exist likelihood-based techniques that apply to any performance evaluation metric, to multiple test sets, and multiple meta-parameter settings. Furthermore, these techniques allow the inclusion of variations in meta-parameter settings or test data into hypothesis testing.

In the mainstream of machine learning research, the questions of validity, reliability, and significance are addressed by exploratory data analysis and descriptive statistics. The goal of our work is to address these questions by **model-based statistical tests** that treat predictions and performance evaluation scores of machine learning models as training data for interpretable machine learning models from the well-understood families of generalized additive models (GAMs) and linear mixed effects models (LMEMs) [Wood, 2017]. We use the term statistical test in a wide sense of basing a decision on a statistic. In the traditional approach to statistical hypothesis testing, a test statistic is computed as a function of observed samples, and used to decide between the null hypothesis and the alternative hypothesis. Model-based statistical tests are based on a probabilistic model for the observed data that incorporates the quantity that we would like to study, i.e., the performance difference of two competing algorithms, as a parameter which is estimated from the data. Such tests are thus formulated in the framework of statistical inference, with the advantage that they allow generalization beyond a concrete evaluation experiment of a machine learning model on a particular test set. Furthermore, the same model-based techniques that are used to analyze predictions of machine learning models can be applied to address the question of validity of data themselves, and to investigate the reliability of human data annotation.

1.2   SCOPE AND OUTLINE OF THIS BOOK

The focus of this book concerns empirical methods that allow for the assessment of the validity, reliability, and significance of prediction processes in NLP and data science. We cover prediction by data annotation, concerning the feature-label relation in the human data annotation process itself, and machine learning prediction, concerning predictions of labels by applications of machine learning models in NLP and data science. The book is organized in three main chapters on the topics of validity, reliability, and significance, respectively. Each chapter is organized by first discussing various theoretical and philosophical aspects of the respective concept. We take inspiration from these theoretical discussions to devise concrete tests that allow for the assessment of the validity, reliability, and significance.

Questions concerning *validity* in machine learning for NLP and data science are discussed in Chapter 2. The point of departure is the problem of whether a machine learning model predicts what it purports to predict. An attempt to formalize this concept has been given in measurement theory for psychological tests: "A test is valid for measuring an attribute if (a) the attribute exists and (b) variations in the attribute causally produce variation in the measurement outcomes" [Borsboom et al., 2004]. For example, a psychological test for developmental stages of children [Inhelder and Piaget, 1958] is valid if children of different ages produce different test results and, conversely, observed outcomes of a valid test can be used to infer the position of children a discrete stages of cognitive development. One might be inclined to think that this notion of validity translates directly into the train-dev-test paradigm. For example, in classification, a "variation in the measurement outcome" is achieved by prediction of a class label, which allows inferring the related "variation in the attribute" if the prediction of a label for an input attribute is accurate. However, this definition is not sufficient to determine validity, as can be best seen with an example. Consider the problem of cross-language information retrieval (CLIR) on patent data. Relevance labels for training and testing in patent CLIR are, in practice, created automatically by using citations in other patents [Graf and Azzopardi, 2008]. Machine learning models such as that of Guo and Gomes [2009] define domain knowledge "attributes," or features, on patent pairs (e.g., same patent class in the International Patent Classification (IPC)) and retrieval score features (e.g., similarity of tf-idf representations), to learn to rank relevant documents higher than irrelevant ones. However, nearly optimal ranking results could be achieved by incorporating patent citations as feature into the learning-to-rank model. This happened in the CLEF-IP 2010 benchmark competition [Piroi and Tait, 2010] where applicant citations extracted from the query document were added to the list of retrieval results in the approach of Magdy and Jones [2010]. Such a model would meet the above sketched validity criterion since the accuracy of predicting relevance labels is nearly perfect. However, there is a further criterion of circularity discussed in philosophy of science that must be avoided. Balzer and Brendel [2019] state that the function to be measured—here the prediction of the learning-to-rank model—and the function that is given—here the known definition of gold standard relevance labels—need to be disjoint. This principle is violated if the citation criteria that are used to define the gold standard labels are incorporated as features in the data representation, and consequently, as features in the machine learning model. For this purpose, we develop a statistical test based on fitting GAMs to feature-label relations in training data or model predictions. This test allows identifying circularity for machine learning data and black-box machine learning models. Chapter 2 will apply this and other tests to assess the validity of machine learning data and machine learning predictions, and illustrate the tests of examples from NLP and data science.

Chapter 3 takes inspiration from the definition of *reliability* in empirical fields, dating back to the works of Fisher [1925, 1935]. In our case, reliability is concerned with the consistency of the prediction of labels by human annotators across replications, or with the consistency of the test data prediction of machine learning models trained under different meta-parameter settings. Let us illustrate our approach on the problem of measuring reliability of machine learning predictions. Our approach is to conduct a variance component analysis [Searle et al., 1992] on random effects of LMEMs that are fitted to performance evaluation data of complex machine learning models. Reliability coefficients can be computed by computing intra-class correlation coefficients [Brennan, 2001, Fisher, 1925] as the ratio of variance attributed to the items of interest, here test sentences, to total variance. Furthermore, Chapter 3 presents a discussion of the shortcomings of chance-corrected agreement metrics like Krippendorff's α, Cohen's κ, or Scott's π that are traditionally used to measure agreement of human annotators in NLP and data science: compared to our approach, where reliability is computed based on variance components of a learned model, these methods are descriptive statistics that compute a single agreement coefficient directly from observed (dis)agreement patterns on categorical variables, with no intent to further analyze the computed coefficient, or to draw conclusion beyond the concrete experiment. We also discuss the advantages and shortcomings of bootstrap estimates of reliability for model predictions. While bootstrap estimates do allow generalization across model predictions under concrete meta-parameter settings, they still do not allow analysis of the reasons for (lacking) reliability. In contrast, a definition of reliability coefficients based on variance components of learned models stresses the importance of a comparison of variance between and within test items. For a machine learning prediction to be reliable, all variance should be explained by differences between test sentences, not by variations within, due to meta-parameter variation, random shuffling of training data, or other inherent randomness of machine learning models. Chapter 3 illustrates these concepts by working through examples for computing reliability coefficients for prediction experiments for NLP and data science tasks.

Chapter 4 addresses the question of the statistical significance of a difference between performance evaluation measurements for predictions in data annotation or in machine learning. The state-of-the-art in statistical significance testing in NLP and data science is an abundance of tests among which a match to individual evaluation metrics has to be found (Dror et al. [2020], Chapter 3), with specialized techniques in order to deal with multiple outputs or multiple datasets (Dror et al. [2020], Chapters 4 and 5, respectively). The goal of our discussion is to reinvigorate likelihood-based techniques for statistical hypothesis testing [Pawitan, 2001] because of their general applicability to any evaluation metric, to multiple test sets, and to multiple meta-parameter settings. The generalized likelihood ratio test (GLRT) dates back to the famous Neyman–Pearson theory [Neyman and Pearson, 1933] and it unfolds its full potential in combination with model-based reliability analysis using LMEMs [Pinheiro and Bates, 2000]: LMEMs trained by maximum likelihood estimation on the performance scores of two machine learning models allow to perform a GLRT that assesses the statistical significance of a difference in performance scores based on the "system" effect of the LMEMs fitted on the performance evaluation data. This is again a model-based approach where the idea of significance testing is based on maximum-likelihood parameter estimators of a probabilistic model. Such a model-based approach allows significance testing of multiple models under a variety of meta-parameter settings and on a concatenation of different test sets, and thus enables the drawing of conclusions beyond a single sample of test data and meta-parameter settings. Chapter 4 introduces the main concepts of statistical significance testing on the example of parametric and sampling-based tests, and discusses and exemplifies the workings of the GLRT on a running example from NLP.

Appendix A presents the mathematical background of the models on which our metrics for measuring validity and reliability are based: GAMs and LMEMs. In order to keep our book self-contained, we introduce the general form of the respective models, present worked-through toy examples that illustrates the concept, and briefly discuss optimization methods to estimate the parameters of the respective models from data.

Throughout the book, we tried to keep the mathematical level accessible to readers from different backgrounds, without sacrificing mathematical rigor. Well known but important theorems are stated explicitly, however, for proofs the reader is referred to the relevant literature. Proof sketches of propositions that build the theoretical basis of the statistical tests proposed in this book are given explicitly.

Furthermore, we provide R code to replicate selected applications of GAMs, LMEMs, and GLRTs that have been presented in the chapters of this book. Code and data are freely available at https://www.cl.uni-heidelberg.de/statnlpgroup/empirical_methods/

1.3   INTENDED READERSHIP

This book is designed for researchers and practitioners whose day-to-day responsibility is experimental work in the area of artificial intelligence, especially applied to NLP and data science problems. Although the book is designed to be self-contained, the section on mathematical background and the rest of the book expect the reader to have some elementary knowledge of statistics and machine learning. Moreover, we expect that the readers bring along some curiosity about problems beyond the boundaries of the train-dev-test paradigm, and are interested in looking beyond the end of their noses, into fields like philosophy of science, psychometrics, or statistics.

While the emphasis of this book is on *model-based* empirical methods, we would like to note that the book also covers traditional approaches from exploratory data analysis to detect validity problems, or standard descriptive statistics on agreement to measure reliability. The goal of the description of traditional techniques is to analyze and understand their shortcomings. However, the respective chapters can also serve as concise and critical introduction into traditional approaches for measuring validity, reliability, and significance.

Last, the focus on applications in NLP and data science expressed in the title of the book should not deter researchers in related fields of artificial intelligence to have a look at the methods proposed in our book. Our running examples are from the area of medical data mining in addition to examples from the area of NLP. Moreover, the fact that similar models are applicable to ranking problems in NLP and information retrieval, or to classification problems for texts and images, or to time series prediction in language modeling and medical diagnostics, invites the application of the same methods for measuring validity, reliability, and significance in various fields of artificial intelligence.

CHAPTER 2

Validity

The notion of validity of a prediction has an ill-defined status in NLP, and it is not associated with a widely accepted evaluation measure such as precision as a measure of prediction quality, or recall as a measure of prediction quantity, in classification. The goal of this chapter is to give a clear definition of the concept of validity in NLP and data science, which then can be operationalized into methods that allow measuring validity, and applied to general NLP and data science tasks.

2.1 VALIDITY PROBLEMS IN NLP AND DATA SCIENCE

First we will present observations on validity issues in NLP and data science that can be found in the literature. These observations have been discussed under the names of dataset bias, information leakage, or circularity, without explicitly referencing to the concept of (in)validity. However, each of the discussed problem areas can be seen as one aspect of a more general problem that we will call the problem of validity.

2.1.1 BIAS FEATURES

A phenomenon frequently discussed in the context of interpretability or trustworthiness of machine learning models is that of superficial patterns in the data which be identified as features that are spuriously, but highly, correlated with target labels. This dataset bias can be due to an annotation bias of crowd workers that adopt certain heuristics to create annotations quickly and efficiently. It may also be triggered by very prominent annotation examples, or by too strict annotation guidelines, that enforce particular annotation heuristics. For example, crowd workers construct contradictions in natural language inference by including negation words in the hypothesis, which allows inferring the contradiction class label without looking at the premise [Gururangan et al., 2018, Poliak et al., 2018]. Similar occurrences of bias features in NLP data have been observed in the form of word-overlap bias for reading comprehension [Jia and Liang, 2017] and natural language inference [McCoy et al., 2019], lexical cues in argument mining [Niven and Kao, 2019], or question types in visual question answering [Agrawal et al., 2018].

The problem of a dataset bias is the fact that minimizing training error leads machine learning models to inherit this bias from the data. The solutions proposed to solve the annotation bias problem include strategies to adversarially manipulate documents in order to distribute bias features across all classes. For example, including distractor sentences using the same words in question and answer avoids an advantage for a simple word overlap bias in question-answering [Jia and Liang, 2017]. Including sentence pairs that use the same words in hypothesis and premise breaks a word overlap bias in natural language inference [McCoy et al., 2019]. Furthermore, resplitting data can break up the correlation between question-type and answer in visual question answering [Agrawal et al., 2018]. Based on such challenge datasets, several machine learning approaches have been proposed to learn robust models that minimize the influence of the bias features [Clark et al., 2019, Kim et al., 2019, Schlegel et al., 2020].

In order to establish a general measure of validity of NLP predictions, we note the nature of the measures that are used to detect superficial cues in the above cited applications. They can be described as normalized co-occurrence statistics of candidate features (e.g., words) and labels (e.g., the class labels of entailment, neutral, and contradiction in natural language inference applications). For example, Poliak et al. [2018] use conditional probability, defined by normalizing the feature-label co-occurrence by the feature occurrence, as measure. Pointwise mutual information as used by Gururangan et al. [2018] normalizes feature-label co-occurrence by feature occurrence times label occurrence. However, these measures will not allow a clear-cut separation of spurious and essential features, i.e., features that are deemed invalid by researchers, and those that are considered "essential to the overall task, so they cannot simply be ignored" [Clark et al., 2019]. Second, we note that in order to deserve the name, a training set bias needs to be computed contrastively on an out-of-domain test set. However, annotation of a challenge test set that is designed to break models based on superficial patterns is sophisticated and costly, and not a standard part of most machine learning datasets.

2.1.2   ILLEGITIMATE FEATURES

A related and even more severe validity problem has been identified in the area of data mining, called data leakage, leading to illegitimate features [Kaufmann et al., 2011]. These are features whose distribution with the target label is heavily skewed so that one illegitimate feature alone is sufficient to predict the correct label. Rosset et al. [2009] give two examples from medical data mining where illegitimate features led to winning systems in benchmark competitions. In one case, patient IDs carried predictive information about the target label of breast cancer. This information was introduced inadvertently by compiling data from different medical institutions, where positive labels were collected exclusively from particular clinical institutions, and negative labels exclusively from others. In another case, diagnosis fields were removed from data, leaving a trace that could be linked directly to target labels.

As solution to this problem, techniques of exploratory data analysis have been suggested, including computing the "difference between estimated and realized out-of-sample performance" [Kaufmann et al., 2011], leading again to the problem of lacking suitable out-of-sample data in most machine learning datasets.

Whereas bias features are legitimate and can and should be part of NLP models, illegitimate features are clear breaches of validity and should be treated differently. This calls first for a clear definition of criteria for validity, and second for automatic methods that allow a clear-cut identification of illegitimate features that should not be used in machine learning.

2.1.3   CIRCULAR FEATURES

Another severe breach of validity in current machine learning research can happen in scenarios where gold standard labels for training and evaluation are created by automatic procedures, without involvement of human annotators. An example is cross-lingual information retrieval for patent prior art search. In this application, relevance ranks are determined from different types of patent citations [Graf and Azzopardi, 2008, Piroi and Tait, 2010]. Patents in the same patent family receive the highest relevance rank, next highest are patents cited in search reports of patent examiners, and the lowest relevance level is assigned to patents cited by patent applicants [Guo and Gomes, 2009, Kuwa et al., 2020, Schamoni and Riezler, 2015]. In such scenarios, the problem of circular features arises if the criteria that are used to define the gold standard labels are incorporated as features in the machine learning model. This happened in the CLEF-IP 2010 benchmark competition [Piroi and Tait, 2010] where applicant citations extracted from the query document were added to the list of retrieval results in the approach of Magdy and Jones [2010]. Because of overlapping citations in the examiner citations and applicant citations, this procedure has been criticized as raising a concern about the validity of the evaluation of the task [Mahdabi and Crestani, 2014].

A similar problem is virulent in machine learning for medical data mining, where clinical measurements are standardly used to define diseases. For example, the systemic inflammatory response syndrome (SIRS) is defined by measuring whether at least two out of four criteria defined in the Surviving Sepsis Campaign Guideline (SSCG)[1] are met. As criticized by Schamoni et al. [2019], these measurements of SIRS criteria are incorporated directly as features in the scoring function, and at the same time used to define a ground truth label, in the approaches of Henry et al. [2015] and Dyagilev and Saria [2016]. In a similar way, Nemati et al. [2018] incorporate all measurements required to identify a change in Sequential Organ Failure Assessment (SOFA) score[2] as features in their prediction function, and simultaneously use them to define a ground truth label of sepsis according to the SOFA-based Sepsis-3 definition [Seymour et al., 2016, Singer et al., 2016]. The same problem of including all defining clinical measurements of the SOFA score as features for machine learning models happened in the data preparation process for the 2019 PhysioNet Challenge on Early Prediction of Sepsis From Clinical Data [Reyna et al., 2019].

The problem of circularity is poorly researched in NLP and data science. A probable reason for this is the focus of the train-dev-test paradigm on operationalizing generalization on unseen data by data splits, either in form of fixed standard splits, random splits [Gorman and

---

[1]The defining criteria concern heart rate (> 90 BPM), temperature (> 38° or < 36°C), respiratory rate (> 20 BPM), or white blood cell count (> 12 or < 4 thousands per microliter), measured in the last 2–8 hours [Dellinger et al., 2013].

[2]The measurements are taken for creatinine level and urine output, Glasgow Coma Scale, bilirubin level, respiratory level, thrombocytes level [Vincent et al., 1996].

Bedrick, 2019], or biased splits [Søgaard et al., 2021]. However, no data splitting technique is able to reveal a circularity problem if the same deterministic function defines the feature-label relation for the whole dataset. Thus, the desideratum regarding circular features is an automatic method for a clear-cut identification of circularity given a single dataset. Circular features also raise ethical concerns if machine learning happens in vital areas such as medical informatics. For example, in machine learning for prediction of sepsis, a disease which causes about 20% of all global deaths [Rudd et al., 2020], it is crucial to develop methods that allow an early identification of circularity problems, before circular machine learning models are applied in real-world scenarios.

2.2   THEORIES OF MEASUREMENT AND VALIDITY

In this section, we will discuss various theoretical considerations on the problem of the validity of a measurement in different empirical sciences. Each approach elaborates certain formal requirements on measurements. Our interest will be to adapt and transfer these formal criteria on the validity of a measurement to a definition of concrete validity checks for machine learning models.

2.2.1   THE CONCEPT OF VALIDITY IN PSYCHOMETRICS

Psychometrics is a field of study concerned with techniques of psychological measurement, i.e., of psychological tests. Classical test theory in psychology [Lord and Novick, 1968] conceptualizes the validity of a psychological test as "criterion validity." It is computed as the correlation of the true test score with an external criterion, where the true score is defined as the expectation of the observed test score.

This view has been revised since Cronbach and Meehl's [1955] introduction of the concept of "construct validity." They argue that tests in psychology are mostly concerned with measuring attributes like intelligence which are not operationally defined criteria—the same is true for attributes like entailment and contradiction in natural language inference, or relevance in information retrieval. Furthermore, they clarify that the status of correlation studies is evidence indicative, but not constitutive, of validity. For example, the fact that height and weight correlate highly in the general population does not qualify weighing a person as a valid measurement of their height. Instead, they introduce the notion of a construct that is defined in an independent theory (called nomological network in Cronbach and Meehl [1955]), and define construct validation as a check if statements in the network lead to predicted relations among observables.

A realist interpretation of Cronbach and Meehl's [1955] account on construct validity is given by Borsboom [2005], Borsboom and Mellenbergh [2007], and Borsboom et al. [2004]. They state:

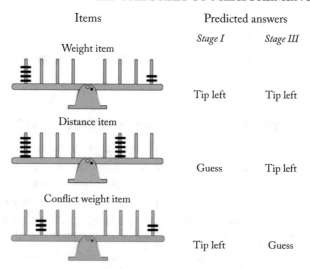

Figure 2.1: Balance scale test for stages of cognitive development. Graphics from Borsboom and Mellenbergh [2007].

> A test is valid for measuring an attribute if and only if (a) the attribute exists and (b) variations in the attribute causally produce variations in the outcomes of the measurement procedure.

A measurement model thus explains how the structure of a theoretical attribute relates to the structure of observations. An example from physics would be a measurement model for temperature that stipulates how the level of mercury in a thermometer systematically relates to temperature. An example from psychology is the test developed by Inhelder and Piaget [1958] to measure stages of cognitive development in children. The test uses a balance scale and asks children to which side the scale will tip. Test situations using different weights on either side and different distances to the pivot point result in different response patterns depending on the developmental stage of the child. Some examples are given in Figure 2.1. In stage I (ages 3–5), children simply choose the side that has most weights. In stage III (ages 10–12), children take distance into account, but only if the weights are equal. In that stage, they start guessing when the weight and distance cues conflict. The relationship between weight and distance is learned only later in early adolescence.

If we relate this example to Borsboom's [2004] above statement about validity, we can say that Inhelder and Piaget's [1958] test for developmental stages of children is valid if different values of the attribute (e.g., children of ages 3–5 vs. 10–12) lead to different test outcomes (corresponding to different cognitive rules concerning weight and distance), and observed outcomes of a valid test can be used to infer the position of children in one of four discrete stages of cognitive development.

For a deeper discussion of more recent issues in test validity theory we refer the reader to Markus and Borsboom [2013].

2.2.2   THE THEORY OF SCALES OF MEASUREMENT

Another approach to measurement theory that also originated in psychometrics is Stevens' [1946] well-known theory of scales of measurement. The notion of a scale is defined as a mathematical representation of empirically observable relations between objects. The task of a researcher is to establish these relations empirically, prove that they can be represented in a formal structure, and find a mapping that is homomorphic to the empirically established relations. The theoretical strategy is to prove the existence and uniqueness of such a homomorphism, and show under which transformations of the scale values this homomorphism is preserved.

Following Stevens [1946], the mathematical group structure of four important scales is defined by the following cumulative operations and scale-specific transformations.

- The nominal scale admits the empirical operation of identification of equality, and it is transformation-invariant under one-to-one substitutions. For example, a numbering of football players allows identifying each individual even after permutation of the numbers.

- The ordinal scale admits the basic empirical operation of rank ordering, and it is transformation-invariant under monotonic maps. For example, the rank-order of the hardness of minerals is preserved under any monotonically increasing function applied to the hardness values.

- The interval scale admits the empirical operation of determination of equality of intervals or differences, but not ratios, between items. It is transformation-invariant under affine linear maps. Examples are the temperature scales of Celsius and Fahrenheit which can be transformed into each other by a affine linear function, where the bias term serves to determine arbitrary zero points.

- The ratio scale allows to determine ratios between items, and it is transformation-invariant under non-affine linear maps. For example, length can be transformed between imperial and metric scale systems by multiplication of each value with a constant.

For our purpose of formalizing a notion of validity, we can tie the criterion of a valid measurement to the effect of transformations of scale values on the predictive power of the representation structure.

Stevens' [1946] theory of measurement has been further developed into the so-called "representational" [Krantz et al., 1971], "axiomatic" [Michell, 2004], or "abstract" [Narens, 1985] measurement theory. For our discussion, the notion of transformation-invariance is crucial, and we refer the reader to the cited textbooks for deeper discussion of more refined representational structures and scales of measurement.

2.2.3   THEORIES OF MEASUREMENT IN PHILOSOPHY OF SCIENCE

According to the view presented in the section above, every measurement yields numerical representations of empirical structures. This type of measurement is called "fundamental" measurement in philosophy of science [Balzer, 1992], and it almost always is found as part of a more complex approach to measurement, called "model-guided" measurement [Balzer and Brendel, 2019]. According to this view, measurement consists in determining a specific function value (called the function value to be measured) from other, given function values (the arguments needed for the calculation), according to a mathematical model. If we think of the mathematical model as a mathematical equation, the determination of a function value to be measured amounts to calculating it from given values by "solving the equation" given by the mathematical model, i.e., by evaluating the corresponding mathematical function for the proper given values.

Let us consider a simple example. Assume that we want to measure the mass of rigid spherical particles by the following setup. We choose one particle p_0 as our reference particle and determine the mass of all the other particles via a unidimensional central collision with p_0. Given that we have velocity readings from both particles before and after the collision, we can determine the mass of the unknown particle (relative to the mass of p_0) by applying the law of conservation of momentum that governs the described physical system. Written more formally, using Balzer and Brendel's [2019] notation, the corresponding measurement model of this procedure is $\langle P, T, \mathbb{R}^+, v, m \rangle$, where

- $p, p_0 \in P$,

- $T = \{t_1, t_2\}$ is a set of two points in time, t_1 before the collision, and t_2 after the collision,

- $v : P \times T \to \mathbb{R}^+$ is the velocity function,

- $m : P \to \mathbb{R}^+$ is the mass function.

- The axioms of the model are

  - *definition of a unit*: $m(p_0) := 1$,

  - *p doesn't move before collision*: $v(p, t_1) = 0$,

- *law of conservation of momentum*:
$$v(p,t_1)m(p) + v(p_0,t_1)m(p_0) = v(p,t_2)m(p) + v(p_0,t_2)m(p_0).$$

The last equation can be solved for $m(p)$, using the axioms of the model, yielding

$$m(p) = \frac{v(p_0,t_1) - v(p_0,t_2)}{v(p,t_2)}. \tag{2.1}$$

The function in Equation (2.1) allows us uniquely determine the mass of a particle (relative to the mass of p_0). Furthermore, as we can see, $m(p)$ depends only on v, which itself is another measurement for which can formulate a measurement model. Such a setting is called a measurement chain. In order to have a proper measurement of the mass of a particle, we thus must also be able to measure v without the need to know m, and we must be able to (practically) determine the necessary quantities for all particles in P. These conditions of unique determination and disjointness of functions are simple cases of two more general conditions on measurement models that can be stated with Balzer and Brendel [2019] as follows.[3]

1. The function to be measured needs to be uniquely determined by the given function(s) and law(s) of the model.

2. The function to be measured and the function that is given need to be disjoint.

The conditions stated above, especially the latter condition of disjointness, can serve as further requirements in our quest of formalizing a notion of validity of predictions.[4]

2.3   PREDICTION AS MEASUREMENT

In the theoretical approaches discussed above, validity was described as a property of a *measurement*. All discussed approaches fundamentally model a measurement process as the determination of a function value for a homomorphic mapping of empirical structures into a numerical system. In the following, we will consider predictions in NLP and data science as instances of measurements. First, we will consider prediction in the form of data annotation, i.e., the assignment of a label y to a complex input $\mathbf{x} \in \mathbb{R}^p$, by either a human annotator or a program following a deterministic rule system. Second, we will look at predictions of machine learning

---

[3]Balzer and Brendel [2019] and Balzer [1992] utilize a formalism that allows them to express all relevant concepts (even functions) in terms of tuples and sets. Essentially, the condition of disjointness of the function to be measured and the function given by the model means that the input measurements must be determinable without knowing the quantity that one wants to measure.

[4]Further and even stricter conditions on validity of measurement are possible and have been discussed in philosophy of science. For example, see Sneed [1971] and Stegmüller [1979, 1986] for a discussion of theoretical terms and possible circularity problems for fundamental measurement procedures. For a deeper discussion of statistical measurement procedures, see Balzer and Brendel [2019].

models, i.e., inference in machine learning where a label $\hat{y}$ is predicted for a complex input $\mathbf{x}$ by a machine learning model. Clearly, both types of predictions can be cast in a functional form: in case of data annotation, the function p is considered deterministic and the prediction is denoted by $y = p(\mathbf{x})$. In the case of prediction by a parametric machine learning model, we specify a parameter vector $\boldsymbol{\theta}$ that refers to the parameters of a trained machine learning model $p_{\boldsymbol{\theta}}$ and the prediction is denoted by $\hat{y}$. In the case of regression, the prediction denotes the score that is assigned to an input such that $\hat{y} = p_{\boldsymbol{\theta}}(\mathbf{x})$. In the case of multi-class classification or structured prediction, we use the maximum a-posteriori prediction where $\hat{y} = \operatorname{argmax}_y p_{\boldsymbol{\theta}}(y|\mathbf{x})$. In both cases of prediction by data annotation or machine learning models, we obtain a functional measurement where y (or $\hat{y}$) is the value of the function p (or $p_{\boldsymbol{\theta}}$) to be measured for a given input $\mathbf{x}$.

2.3.1   FEATURE REPRESENTATIONS

Our notion of features $\mathbf{x}$ refers to *raw* input features, i.e., feature representations that exist external to and independent of machine learning models which take them as input data. Clearly, raw features can be complex measurements themselves, or in the words of Gitelman [2013]: "raw data" is an oxymoron. For example, in medical data science, features consist of complex and derived measurements of vital signals (respiratory rate, heart rate, blood pressure, etc.), laboratory test results (blood urea nitrogen, hematocrit, creatinine, etc.), and clinical information (clinical history, ICD-9 codes, etc.) [Schamoni et al., 2019]. Even in NLP, raw representations of text data are the result of an explicit generation procedure that is standard for the specific scientific discipline. For example, in cross-lingual patent retrieval, standard feature representations include identities of characters or words in the textual part of a patent file, but also meta-information like patent number, patent family identifier, or the patent numbers of cited prior-art patents. What makes meta-information features such as citations in patent retrieval [Magdy and Jones, 2010] or patient IDs in medical data science [Rosset et al., 2009] especially interesting is the fact that they can be (mis)used in unintended ways and thus play a central role in validity testing.[5]

Our choice of feature representations is motivated by the fact that every theoretical approach to validity discussed above assumes an a-priori reference point relative to which validity of a measurement is determined. Such a reference point is called "attribute" [Borsboom et al., 2004], "empirical structure" [Stevens, 1946], or "given function" [Balzer, 1992], in the respective approaches, however, they all are *interpretable*[6] feature representations. This connects our work to related work on explanatory machine learning that has to recur to interpretable feature representations once it comes to the actual explanation of the workings of deep learning models. For example, Ribeiro et al. [2016] conceptualizes interpretable feature representations

---

[5]A well-known example from the area of image processing is the (mis)use of copyright tags in image processing [Lapuschkin et al., 2019].

[6]A precise definition of the notion of interpretability is an open research problem that is outside the scope of this book. It involves issues ranging from the (non)concurvity of features [Amodio et al., 2014, Tomaschek et al., 2018] to human factors of intelligibility [Alvarez-Melis and Jaakkola, 2018, Doshi-Velez and Kim, 2017, Miller, 2017].

for text applications as binary vectors indicating the presence or absence of words or characters in a lexicon or alphabet. If techniques like layer-wise relevance propagation (LRP) are applied to text data [Ding et al., 2017], activation patterns in neural networks are eventually mapped to discrete words. Furthermore, no matter how text data are represented internally in neural networks—by continuous-valued vector representations that are pre-trained, e.g., by recurrent neural networks [Mikolov et al., 2013], convolutional neural nets [Kim, 2014], or bi-directional transformers [Devlin et al., 2019], or learned as weights of a dedicated layer during training of a task-specific loss function [Collobert et al., 2011]—there always exists a raw input data representation that is external to the neural network model and can be reconstructed from the internal embedding representation.[7]

2.3.2   MEASUREMENT DATA

Before we define the validity of a data annotation or machine learning prediction, a further simplification will be helpful. Let us start with the case of human data annotation: we note that in order to assess the validity of a prediction in form of a data annotation, we are interested in the resulting assignment of a label y to an input $\mathbf{x}$, and we consider the actual system that performed the annotation, i.e., the human annotator or the rule system, as fixed and deterministic, thus we can disregard it. For cases of data annotation, the question of the validity of a prediction can therefore be reduced to the question of validity of the functional relation of a feature x_k to a label y, where x_k denotes a component of a p-dimensional feature vector $\mathbf{x} = (x_1, x_2, \ldots, x_p)$, and we obtain a dataset $D = \{(\mathbf{x}^n, y^n)\}_{n=1}^N$ of feature-label relations whose validity can be analyzed by the descriptive and model-based techniques presented in the following sections.

Examples for predictions in these sections will be taken from the NLP area of cross-language information retrieval, and from the data science field of medical informatics. For text-based applications such as cross-language information retrieval, $\mathbf{x}$ can be seen as vectors of words or characters, and y can be seen as ordinal numbers indicating a relevance level. For a medical diagnosis, $\mathbf{x}$ consists of clinical measurements such as heart rate, body temperature, or bilirubin level. Labels y can again be thought of as ordinal numbers denoting severity levels. All prediction models discussed in this chapter are neural networks trained with regression loss.

Similar to the case of data annotation, in order to define the validity of a machine learning prediction on the basis of features and labels, we are not interested in the actual machine learning model p_θ that performed the prediction, but only in the resulting prediction of a label $\hat{y}$ for an input $\mathbf{x}$. Our idea of transferring the knowledge of a neural network into a dataset of inputs and predicted labels is inspired by knowledge distillation [Hinton et al., 2015, Kim and Rush, 2016, Tan et al., 2018]. The original goal of knowledge distillation is to map a complex neural network to a simpler model by treating the complex model as teacher for the simpler student model. Similar to data annotation, we would like to disregard the peculiarities of the prediction system,

---

[7]In a similar way, factorized latent representations [Chen et al., 2016, Higgins et al., 2017, Locatello et al., 2019] have to be mapped to interpretable concepts when used as explanatory factors in image processing.

i.e., the teacher model q_{θ_T}, and reduce the question of validity of machine learning predictions to the question of validity of the functional relation of input features x_k in $\mathbf{x} = (x_1, x_2, \ldots, x_p)$ to teacher predictions $\hat{y}$. In case of regression, we obtain the prediction $\hat{y}$ for an input $\mathbf{x}$ as the real-valued score $q_{\theta_T}(\mathbf{x})$. In case of logistic regression, the teacher model score $q_{\theta_T}(y|\mathbf{x})$ can be thresholded to predict positive or negative classes. In case of multi-class classification or structured prediction, the maximum a-posteriori prediction $\hat{y} = \mathrm{argmax}_y \, q_{\theta_T}(y|\mathbf{x})$ can be used. In any case, we obtain a dataset $D = \{(\mathbf{x}^n, y^n)\}_{n=1}^{N}$ where $y^n = \hat{y}^n$ for $i = 1, \ldots, n$, that can be used to train a student model.

This representation allows us to assess the problem of validity of a prediction by model inference without knowledge of the data on which the machine learning model in question was trained. All we need to know is the predictions of the model, together with an intelligible set of input features. A further advantage of this representation is that it allows us to treat prediction by data annotation and by model inferences from the same formal perspective, namely as validity of the functional relation of input features to labels in a dataset.

2.4   DESCRIPTIVE AND MODEL-BASED VALIDITY TESTS

Inspired by the theoretical accounts on measurement and validity presented in Section 2.2, and with a focus on the types of invalid features discussed in Section 2.1, we propose the following necessary conditions for validity of a prediction in NLP and data science. If a prediction is valid, then none of the invalidity criteria stated below must apply.

> **Definition 2.1 (Validity).**   The functional relationship between a feature and a label in a prediction by data annotation by or machine learning inference is **invalid** if at least one of the following conditions holds:
>
> 1. the correlation between the feature and labels varies substantially across datasets from different domains (**dataset bias**),
>
> 2. the predictive power of the feature is dependent on a transformation of its scale representation (**scale transformation**), and
>
> 3. the feature allows an exact reconstruction of a deterministic target functional definition while nullifying the contribution of all other features (**circularity**).

In the following, we will support each condition by an operational definition that is based on a statistical test for the respective criterion.

2.4.1 DATASET BIAS TEST

Dataset bias can be described as the problem of when a model learns superficial patterns in the data to perform well on training data, but does not generalize well and performs poorly on out-of-domain test data [Clark et al., 2019]. In order to identify such superficial patterns, here called bias features, a contrast of a measure between in-domain and out-of-domain data is required. Here we identify bias features as those features in a set of given candidates that are correlated with the class label on the training set from one domain, but are uncorrelated or anti-correlated with the label on a test set from another domain.

Testing for invariance of correlations between features and target labels across datasets from different domains can be motivated by an invariance criterion that is entailed by the central principle of independent mechanisms in causal inference [Pearl, 2009, Peters et al., 2017, Schölkopf et al., 2021]. Techniques like Invariant Causal Prediction [Peters et al., 2016] or Invariant Risk Minimization [Arjovsky et al., 2019] promote learning correlations that are invariant across distinct, separate training environments so that the will also hold in novel testing environments. It is suggested that such invariant features relate to the causal explanations themselves,[8] so they allow us to connect the concept of invariance of correlations across domains with the concept of validity presented by Borsboom et al. [2004]: recall their notion from Section 2.2.1 stating that a test is valid for measuring an attribute if and only if (a) the attribute exists and (b) variations in the attribute causally produce variations in the outcomes of the measurement procedure. Using the concept of domain invariant feature representations, our dataset bias test can be seen as a check whether the functional relation of features (our "attributes") and labels (our "measurement outcomes") is invalid, by testing whether the correlation of feature values to label values varies across domains (our replacement for the notion of "(non)causality").

Let us formalize a dataset bias test using the standard notion of the Pearson sample correlation coefficient (see Larsen and Marx [2012]).

> **Definition 2.2 (Dataset Bias Test).** Given a dataset of feature-label relations $D = \{(\mathbf{x}^n, y^n)\}_{n=1}^N$, the **sample correlation coefficient** $R(x_k, y, D)$ for a feature x_k in $\mathbf{x} = (x_1, x_2, \ldots, x_p)$ and a label y in dataset D is computed

---

[8]Clearly, invariance of correlations across different environments is only part of causality, and further conditions are necessary [Rosenfeld et al., 2021]. Thus, we do not make any causality claims on our validity tests, but instead we take a practical approach where computing the descriptive statistics of the correlation coefficient for given features and labels across given domains replaces the notion of causality in Borsboom and Mellenbergh's approach to construct validity.

as

$$R(x_k, y, D) = \frac{\mathbb{E}(x_k y) - \mathbb{E}(x_k)\mathbb{E}(y)}{\sqrt{\mathbb{V}(x_k)}\sqrt{\mathbb{V}(y)}},$$

where $\mathbb{E}(x_k) = \frac{1}{n}\sum_{n=1}^{N} x_k^n$, $\mathbb{E}(y) = \frac{1}{N}\sum_{i=1}^{n} y^n$, $\mathbb{E}(x_k y) = \frac{1}{N}\sum_{n=1}^{N} x_k^n y^n$, $\mathbb{V}(x_k) = \frac{1}{N}\sum_{n=1}^{N}(x_k^n - \mathbb{E}(x_k))^2$, and $\mathbb{V}(y) = \frac{1}{N}\sum_{n=1}^{N}(y^n - \mathbb{E}(y))^2$.

A feature x_k exhibits a **dataset bias** for an in-domain dataset D_{ID} if $R(x_k, y, D_{\text{ID}})$ substantially differs from $R(x_k, y, D_{\text{OOD}})$ for an out-of-domain dataset D_{OOD}.

The test described in Definition 2.2 computes a linear correlation between two random variables, representing feature and label, and assesses a dataset bias if the difference in correlation between to datasets exceeds a certain threshold which is to be set by the user.

Let us consider the NLP task of natural language inference as an example. This task is defined as follows: for a pair of natural language sentences (premise and hypothesis), a prediction has to be made whether the hypothesis is true given the premise (entailment), false (contradiction), or unrelated (neutral). McCoy et al. [2019] give an example for a bias feature based on lexical overlap that predicts entailment for any hypothesis whose words all appear in the premise:

(1) *Premise:* The judge was paid by the actor.
     Hypothesis: The actor paid the judge.

(2) *Premise:* The actor was paid by the judge.
     Hypothesis: The actor paid the judge.

While this bias feature predicts entailment correctly for example (1), it fails on example (2). Bias features like lexical overlap for natural language inference tasks have been described in several publications (see Schlegel et al. [2020] for an overview). In the following, we will apply the dataset bias test described above to a set of seven feature templates on premise (pre) and hypothesis (hyp), shown in Table 2.1.[9]

As the in-domain training set, we use the multi-genre natural language inference (MNLI) dataset [Williams et al., 2018], consisting of 392,287 sentence pairs[10] with entailment information. As the in-domain test set, we use 9,630 sentence pairs that were filtered from the matched test examples provided in the MNLI dataset. As the out-of-domain test sets, we use the challenge dataset called HANS [McCoy et al., 2019] and the Adversarial NLI (ANLI) dataset [Nie et al., 2020]. The HANS dataset consists of 30,000 sentence pairs that were created

---

[9]Rescaling was performed by the min-max formula $f(x) = \frac{x-\min}{\max-\min}$. Negations were computed by a regular expression extracting negation words, following https://www.nltk.org/_modules/nltk/sentiment/util.html.

[10]415 sentence pairs were filtered out because of duplications or missing labels.

Table 2.1: Feature templates for natural language inference

	Template	Meaning	Range
(1)	hyp-is-subseq	hyp is sub-sequence of pre	{0, 1}
(2)	all-in-pre	all words in hyp are in pre	{0, 1}
(3)	percent-in-pre	percent of words of hyp in pre	[0, 1]
(4)	scaled-len-diff	rescaled log-length difference	[0, 1]
(5)	cos-sim	rescaled cosine similarity	[0, 1]
(6)	pre-has-neg	negation in pre	{0, 1}
(7)	hyp-has-neg	negation in hyp	{0, 1}

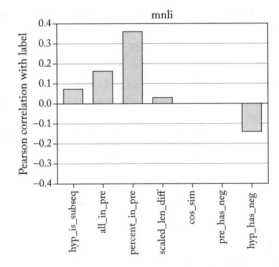

Figure 2.2: Sample correlation between features and gold labels on MNLI training set.

purposely such that models will fail on a particular subset of the data, if certain superficial heuristics are used. The heuristics used correspond to our templates hyp-is-subseq, all-in-pre, percent-in-pre, and a third constituent overlap heuristics based on parsing that is not used in our experiment. For each heuristic, half of the examples can be correctly classified using the heuristic and half of them can not. The second out-of-domain test set consists of 1,200 examples that were created by human annotators as part of the ANLI data set. The annotators were instructed to provide a hypothesis that fools the model into misclassifying the label. This annotation process was repeated by retraining the model on the hard examples, and the overall adversarial human-in-the-loop procedure was iterated for three rounds.

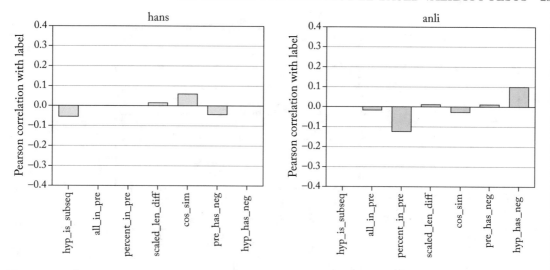

Figure 2.3: Sample correlation between features and gold labels on HANS and ANLI data.

For comparability, we mapped all datasets to binary classification, with entailment as positive class, and neutral and contradiction comprising the negative class. Figure 2.2 shows the Pearson sample correlation coefficient computed for the seven feature templates on the MNLI dataset. We see that the three overlap features are positively correlated with the positive label entailment, while a negation in the hypothesis is correlated with the negative class.

Figure 2.3 shows the sample correlation coefficient computed on the HANS and ANLI datasets. The templates for lexical overlap are constants by construction in the HANS dataset, yielding zero covariance with the label, which justifies the attribution of zero correlation in these cases. The other templates are non-constant and show a small correlation to the labels. A different pattern is visible for the ANLI data, with overlap and negation templates having an opposite effect than in the MNLI data, due to their adversarial construction. According to our definition above, a case of dataset bias can be assessed for all templates (except scaled-len-diff) if "substantial difference" in correlation is defined as the difference between no correlation, positive correlation, and negative correlation.

Next, we consider a case where we train a BERT deep neural network [Devlin et al., 2019] on the MNLI training set, and evaluate its predictions on test data from a different domain. The sample correlation coefficient shown in Figure 2.4 is computed on the relation of features to predicted labels on MNLI data. Comparing Figure 2.4 to Figure 2.2 shows that a very similar pattern can be found for correlations between features and gold-standard labels and and correlations between features and predicted labels. Figure 2.5 shows that the dataset bias that the model has picked up on the MNLI data is transferred to the HANS data, and even more prominently, to the ANLI data. However, the accuracy results in Table 2.2 show that the

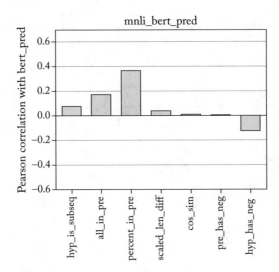

Figure 2.4: Sample correlation between features and model predicted labels on MNLI data.

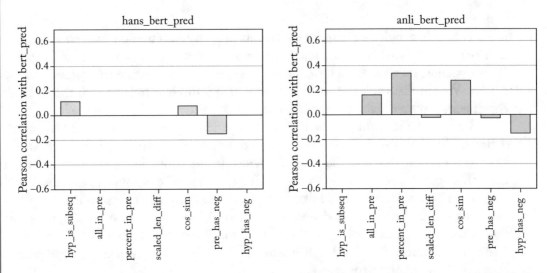

Figure 2.5: Sample correlation between features and model predicted labels on HANS and ANLI data.

dataset bias negatively affects model accuracy by around 50% when evaluating the MNLI-biased model on out-of-domain data like HANS or ANLI.

Discussion. The dataset bias test described above is a descriptive statistic that computes and compares the sample correlation coefficients of variables that are assumed to be linearly or

Table 2.2: Accuracy for natural language inference of MNLI-trained BERT model

	MNLI Train	MNLI Test	HANS Test	ANLI Test
Accuracy	0.98	0.91	0.54	0.58

monotonically correlated. Since the test measures a bias toward idiosyncrasies of a particular in-domain dataset, a necessary prerequisite for the test is the existence of a designated out-of-domain dataset for a comparative evaluation of feature-label correlations. However, sophisticated and costly annotation of adversarial datasets is not part of the standard package of machine learning datasets.

Furthermore, dataset bias is a never-ending problem that can only be solved by never-ending learning [Mitchell et al., 2015]. For example, a dataset bias might exist at certain moment for a given pair of datasets, and the bias in question may be resolved by data improvement and joint training procedures such as those proposed by Clark et al. [2019], Kim et al. [2019], McCoy et al. [2019], and Nie et al. [2020], yet a new bias can be detected anytime against any new unseen out-of-domain dataset. In other words, an extensional definition of the notion of domain on which the dataset bias test is based is a moving target. The same is true of the notion of environment [Arjovsky et al., 2019, Peters et al., 2016] on which the motivating concept of invariant causal prediction is based. Since there are no clear criteria for differentiating domains or environments, theoretical justifications or causal interpretations of the dataset bias test have to be made very cautiously.

Last, what makes this test unattractive as a validity metric is the fact that there is not clear-cut threshold for correlation coefficients to assess invalidity, and no single correlation measure that would be applicable to all cases of suspected dataset bias.[11]

2.4.2   TRANSFORMATION INVARIANCE TEST

The transformation invariance test directly incorporates the ideas of Stevens' [1946] theory of scales of measurement described in Section 2.2.2 into a statistical test. In practice, we apply the idea of permissible scale transformations to feature representations in a given dataset, and check if the predictions of a machine learning model that is trained on these data are not affected by applying permissible transformations to any feature in the data. That is, any evaluation metric applied the predictions of two models trained on the same data should yield the same result, with or without applying admissible feature transformations.

Formally, the mathematical groups defining scale representations are subgroups of each other, with the ratio group being a subgroup of the interval group, which itself is a subgroup of

---

[11]For example, correlation in multi-class classification problems requires measures such as mutual information [Cover and Thomas, 1991], and even our natural language inference example used a special subcase of Pearson correlation called point-biserial correlation between continuous and dichotomous variables [Agresti, 2002].

the ordinal group, which is a subgroup of the nominal group. Thus, the nominal group permits the most transformations, while the ratio group permits the least. A statistical test based on permissible transformations can then be stated as follows:

Definition 2.3 (Transformation Invariance Test).   The structure of the representation of an input feature x_k in $\mathbf{x} = (x_1, x_2, \ldots, x_p)$ needs to be transformation invariant under an operation $T(x_k)$, where

- the **nominal** scale representation permits **one-to-one substitutions** $T(x_k)$,

- the **ordinal** scale representation permits mappings by **strictly monotonic increasing functions** $T(x_k)$,

- the **interval** scale representation permits mappings by **affine linear functions** $T(x_k) = ax_k + b$, for $a \in \mathbb{R}^+ \setminus \{0\}$, $b \in \mathbb{R}$, and

- the **ratio** scale representation permits mappings by **non-affine linear functions** $T(x_k) = ax_k$, for $a \in \mathbb{R}^+ \setminus \{0\}$.

Given a training set $D = \{(\mathbf{x}^n, y^n)\}_{n=1}^N$ of features and gold standard labels, **transformation invariance** is violated if applying permissible transformations to any feature x_k in $\mathbf{x}^n = (x_1, x_2, \ldots, x_p)$, $\forall n = 1, \ldots, N$ changes the predictions of a machine learning model trained on D.

An example for a violation of transformation invariance, leading to invalidity, can be seen in the use of patient IDs as feature, which has been described as "illegitimate" by Kaufmann et al. [2011]. The reason for this illegitimate use of features is described as a case of "information leakage" that happened at the KDD Cup 2008 data science competition in Rosset et al. [2009]. The exploratory analysis of the data presented by Rosset et al. [2009] is illustrated in Figure 2.6. It shows the distribution of labels, with black dots indicating malignant candidates and gray dots indicating benign cases of cancer, against patient IDs (in log scale on x-axis). This distribution allows a binning into five ranges of consecutive IDs where the vast majority of malignant cases is in the first bin (IDs 0 to 20,000) and fourth bin (IDs 4,000,000–4,870,000). Rosset et al. [2009] report that the binning and its correlation with the labels generalized from training to test data. Furthermore, the score distribution (shown on the y-axis) of a linear SVM trained on 117 features demonstrates that the model is able to learn a relatively clear decision boundary between positive and negative labels from these data. Rosset et al. [2009] hypothesize that this illegitimate information was inadvertently introduced by compiling data from different medi-

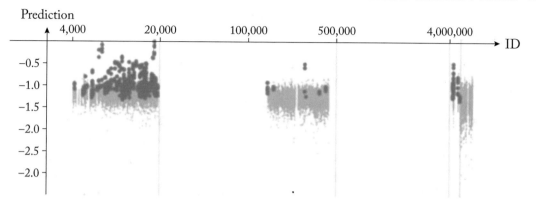

Figure 2.6: Distribution of malignant (black dots) and benign (gray dots) cases of cancer labels against patient IDs (in log-scale on x-axis), with predictions scores of an SVM model trained on the data (on y-axis). Graphics from Rosset et al. [2009].

cal institutions, and by collecting positive and negative labels from particular institutions with consecutive patient IDs.

Irrespective of the origin of the information leakage, a clear-cut criterion to detect this case of invalidity is an application of the transformation invariance test for nominally scaled variables. Patient IDs constitute an assignment of numerals according to the rule that one should not assign the same numeral to different patients, or different numerals to the same patient. Furthermore, the empirical operation of the determination of equality by an assignment of an ID should be invariant to the transformational operation of permutations. A transformation invariance test for nominally scaled variables would apply the operation of permutation to patient IDs, however, exactly this operation would defeat the predictive power of the feature in the example of Rosset et al. [2009] since the binning in Figure 2.6 that could be used to predict labels on the test data would no longer be possible. Thus, a breach of validity can be assessed according to our criterion that the predictive power of the feature must be independent of a transformation of its scale representation.

Discussion.   The status of the transformation invariance test as a validity metric is that of a descriptive tool from exploratory data analysis that applies to specific feature representations and models trained on them. Clearly, the validity problem introduced by the patient ID feature in the example above could also be detected as an instance of a dataset bias, by comparing the sample correlation coefficient of this feature to the labels on the KDD Cup 2008 data to the sample correlation coefficient on any other data. Such a relative comparison would inherit all problems of finding the right correlation measure, of capturing nonlinear associations, and of choosing appropriate thresholds that plague the dataset bias test. If applicable, the transformation invariance test allows for a clear assessment of a breach of validity. However, the obvious shortcoming of this test is the limited number of cases where validity problems are due to violations of scale representations.

2.4.3   A MODEL-BASED TEST FOR CIRCULARITY

The notion of circularity in this work is inspired by the discussion of validity in philosophy of science given in Section 2.2.3. A central requirement on measurement theories stated by Balzer and Brendel [2019] is that the function to be measured—for example, the function expressed by a machine learning model $p_\theta(\mathbf{x})$ that predicts a label $\hat{y}$ for a given input feature representation $\mathbf{x}$—and the function that is given—for example, the assignment of a gold standard label y to an input $\mathbf{x}$ by a deterministic functional definition $p(\mathbf{x})$—need to be disjoint. This principle is violated if the criteria that are used to define the gold standard labels are incorporated as features in the data representation, and consequently, as features in the machine learning model. As the experiments presented below show, including measurements that are deterministically related to the target labels as input features to machine learning leads to a circularity in prediction where the machine learning model learns nothing else but to reconstruct the known functional definition. Based on a machine reconstruction of the known target definition, machine learning yields perfect predictions which break down on real-world data where the target-defining measurements may not or only incompletely be available.

In the following section we present a circularity test that shows, for given datasets and black-box machine learning models, whether the target functional definition can be reconstructed from input feature representations, or whether it has been used in training a machine learning model. We will exemplify the notion of circular features with instances from medical data mining and from cross-lingual information retrieval. In contrast to the descriptive statistics of the dataset bias test and the transformation invariance test, the circularity test takes a model-based approach. This means that the test applies techniques of machine learning itself by fitting interpretable probabilistic models from the well-understood family of generalized additive models to data annotation and model prediction experiments, and by performing statistical tests on the fitted models. Furthermore, the circularity test does not require a designated out-of-domain dataset for comparative evaluation, but rather it can be applied to a single dataset.

GAMs, Deviance, and Nullification

The first prerequisite of a model-based circularity test is the availability of an expressive and yet interpretable model fitted to data $D = \{(\mathbf{x}^n, y^n)\}_{n=1}^N$ resulting from a data annotation or model prediction process. We start with distributional assumptions on our modeling approach. The standard assumption is that the deviations of the response variable Y^n around its mean $\mu^n = \mathbb{E}[Y|\mathbf{x}^n]$ are Gaussian with variance σ^2:

$$Y^n - \mu^n = \epsilon^n, \text{ where } \epsilon^n \sim \mathcal{N}(0, \sigma^2) \text{ for } n = 1, \ldots, N. \tag{2.2}$$

As a model for μ, we adopt the highly expressive and yet interpretable class of *Generalized Additive Models* (GAMs) that originated in the area of biostatistics [Hastie and Tibshirani, 1990] to circumvent the restriction of strictly linear features in generalized linear regression models. The key idea of GAMs is decomposing a multivariate function into a sum of functions with lower dimensional inputs, called *feature shapes*, which are learned from the data. The one-dimensional feature shapes $f_k(x_k)$ for each feature x_k (or pairs of features (x_i, x_j)) in $\mathbf{x} = (x_1, x_2, \ldots, x_p)$ are additively combined and can be nonlinear functions themselves. The model is intelligible since the contribution of each feature x_k to the prediction can be interpreted by visualizing feature shapes via plotting $f_k(x_k)$ against x_k, especially for one- or two-dimensional features shapes. The general form of a GAM assumes Y to be a random variable from the exponential family, and $g(\cdot)$ to be a nonlinear link function:

$$g(\mu) = \sum_{k=1}^{p} f_k(x_k) + \sum_{i \neq j} f_{ij}(x_i, x_j). \tag{2.3}$$

The additive Gaussian error model is recovered by using the identity link function $g(\mu) = \mu$, and specifying the distribution of Y^n to be of the Gaussian subclass of the exponential family:

$$Y^n = \sum_{k=1}^{p} f_k(x_k^n) + \sum_{i \neq j} f_{ij}(x_i^n, x_j^n) + \epsilon^n, \text{ where } \epsilon^n \sim \mathcal{N}(0, \sigma^2) \text{ for } n = 1, \ldots, N. \tag{2.4}$$

In the following examples, feature shapes are modeled by regression *spline* functions. For mathematical background on modeling with splines and on estimation of GAMs we refer the reader to Appendix A.1.

The first part of our statistical test for circularity based on GAMs is a measure for the fit of the model to the data $D = \{(\mathbf{x}^n, y^n)\}_{n=1}^{N}$. We will use the likelihood-based criterion of *scaled deviance* of a model for this purpose. McCullagh and Nelder [1989] define it as a metric proportional to the difference between the log-likelihood $\ell(\mu)$ of a model μ to the log-likelihood ℓ^* of the saturated model, i.e., to the model in the distributional family that achieves the highest possible likelihood value given the data:

$$D_{\mu}^* = 2(\ell^* - \ell(\mu)). \tag{2.5}$$

The saturated model corresponds to an exact fit by setting the fitted values equal to the observed data, thus it does not depend on parameters. The distribution of a single observation of the additive Gaussian model with known variance σ^2 is

$$p(y^n | \mu^n, \sigma^2) = \frac{1}{\sqrt{2\pi\sigma^2}} \exp\left(-\frac{(y^n - \mu^n)^2}{2\sigma^2}\right), \tag{2.6}$$

with log-likelihood

$$\ell(\mu^n) = -\frac{1}{2}\log(2\pi\sigma^2) - \frac{(y^n - \mu^n)^2}{2\sigma^2}. \tag{2.7}$$

Setting $\mu^n = y^n$ in the saturated model yields $\ell^* = -\frac{1}{2}\log(2\pi\sigma^2)$ so that

$$D_\mu^* = 2(\ell^* - \ell(\mu)) = \frac{(y^n - \mu^n)^2}{\sigma^2}. \tag{2.8}$$

Apart from the scaling factor σ^2, this metric is identical to the residual sum of squares R^2, which is a standard measure of model fit in statistics. Following Hastie and Tibshirani [1986], we use the *percentage of deviance explained* to make the metric more interpretable, and denote it by D^2 in analogy to R^2:

$$D^2(\mu) = 1 - \frac{D_\mu^*}{D_{\mu_0}}, \tag{2.9}$$

where D_{μ_0} is the deviance for the model μ_o that uses just a constant intercept term (without any predictor variables) for all response variables, yielding $D^2(\cdot) \in [0, 1]$.

The intended usage of the D^2 metric in a circularity test on a given dataset $D = \{(\mathbf{x}^n, y^n)\}_{n=1}^N$ is to train a set of GAMs, one for each member of the powerset of features, and to find the model with maximal D^2 and smallest degrees of freedom.[12]

In addition to this metric, we employ a second check to differentiate input features that are deterministically related to the labels in the data from possible additional features in the input data that are irrelevant to the label-defining function. Here we make use of the consistency property of the maximum likelihood estimator used to fit GAMs (see Wood [2017]).

Definition 2.4 (Consistency). Let $M := \{p_\theta : \theta \in \Theta\}$ be a parametric statistical model where $\theta \mapsto p_\theta$ is injective. Further, let $p_{\theta_0} \in M$ denote the true model of the data generating process for a dataset $D = \{(\mathbf{x}^n, y^n)\}_{n=1}^N$. Then an estimator θ_N is called *consistent* iff for all $\epsilon > 0$ holds

$$P\left(|\theta_N - \theta_0| > \epsilon\right) \xrightarrow{N \to \infty} 0.$$

Given the true model of the data generation process, the consistency property of GAMs allows us to identify circular features as those that approximate the data generating process with a non-zero feature shape, and features that are not related to the data generation process as those with constant zero feature shapes.

Proposition 2.5 (Nullification). *Let $p_{\theta_N}^{GAM}$ be a GAM that optimizes the likelihood of data $D = \{(\mathbf{x}^n, y^n)\}_{n=1}^N$ that have been produced by a deterministic data labeling function $p : \mathbf{x}^n \to y^n$, $n = 1, \ldots, N$. Furthermore, assume that p can be approximated by a model $M^{GAM} = \{p_\theta^{GAM} : \theta \in \Theta\}$.*

---

[12]In the simplest form, degrees of freedom of a model are calculated by the number of tuneable parameters. For example, a GAM for $n = 1, \ldots, N$ data points, modeling feature shapes for each of $k = 1, \ldots, p$ input features with cubic splines of d_k parameters for each feature, together with a smoothness penalty for each of feature, adds up to $(N \times \sum_{k=1}^p d_k) + p$ degrees of freedom. For the notion of *effective degrees of freedom* and its computation, see Appendix A.1.

Then any feature x_k with a non-zero contribution to the deterministic labeling function $p(x_k)$ will have a non-zero feature shape $f(x_k)$, and any other feature $x_j, j \neq k$ in the feature set will have a feature shape of a constant zero function, with a probability that converges to 1 as the sample size increases.

Proof sketch. The proposition follows directly from the consistency of maximum likelihood estimators for GAMs. This has been shown, for example, by Heckman [1986] for GAMs based on cubic regression splines. By consistency, the maximum likelihood estimator θ_N will converge in probability to the data generating parameters θ_0. Since the model $M^{\text{GAM}} = \{p_\theta^{\text{GAM}} : \theta \in \Theta\}$ is identifiable, by the injectivity of the mapping $\theta \mapsto p_\theta$, the data generating parameters θ_0 will identify the data generating model $p_{\theta_0}^{\text{GAM}}$. By the additive structure of this model, only features determining the feature-label relations in the data $D = \{(\mathbf{x}^n, y^n)\}_{n=1}^N$ have non-zero feature shapes, and the feature shapes of all other features in the feature set have constant zero values. $\square$

The criterion expressed in Proposition 2.5 will be called the *nullification* criterion. Based on interpretable models in form of GAMs, the D^2 metric, and the nullification criterion, we define a circularity test that proceeds by searching for the model with highest deviance and lowest degrees of freedom over the powerset of features, and by confirming that all other features except the ones found in the first step are nullified.

Definition 2.6 (Circularity Test). Given a dataset of feature-label relations $D = \{(\mathbf{x}^n, y^n)\}_{n=1}^N$ where $\mathbf{x}^n = (x_1, x_2, \ldots, x_p)$ is a p-dimensional feature vector, let $C \subseteq \mathcal{P}(\{1, \ldots, p\})$ indicate the set of candidate circular features in dataset D, and let $\mathcal{M}_C := \{\mu_c : c \in C\}$ be the set of models obtained by fitting a GAM based on feature set c to the data D. A set of **circular features** c^* is detected by applying the following two-step test.

1. $c^* = \text{argmax}_{c \in C} \, D^2(\mu_c)$ where $D^2(\mu_{c^*})$ is close to 1, and in case the maximizer is not unique, the maximizer is chosen whose associated GAM μ_{c^*} has the smallest degrees of freedom.

2. The feature shapes of every feature $x_j : j \in \{1, \ldots, p\}$
   c^* added to the GAM μ_{c^*} is nullified in the resulting model.

Note that identifiability and consistency of maximum likelihood estimators is an essential property of spline-based GAMs as described in Hastie and Tibshirani [1990], Heckman [1986], and Wood [2017]. This is not necessarily true of neural network-based neural additive models (NAMs) [Agarwal et al., 2020], for which identifiability or consistency has not been shown.

Furthermore, note that the circularity test defined above is not restricted to single features, but it allows assessing the circularity of feature sets by fitting and testing the deviance and nullification of multivariate GAMs. We will present an example from medical data science below where the functional definition of the target label is based on a combination of two variables. Last, note that a useful practice to specify the set of candidate circular features in Definition 2.6 is to sort the features by their bivariate feature-label correlation. As will be illustrated in the examples below, while the feature-label correlation is not sufficient to make a clear-cut distinction between circular and non-circular features, it allows sorting circular features before non-circular features and thus it can avoid the computational cost of training a separate GAM on each member of the powerset of features.

Circularity in Data Annotation

In the following examples, we assume that we have access to a dataset $D = \{(\mathbf{x}^n, y^n)\}_{n=1}^{N}$ of input features $\mathbf{x} = (x_1, x_2, \ldots, x_p)$ and gold standard labels y. Our goal is to investigate if the dataset includes features that allow an exact reconstruction of the target functional definition. Since machine learning models optimized to minimize training error will directly inherit such features, a circularity test should be applied that detects such features before they are applied for machine learning predictions in real-world scenarios.

Circularity in Patent Prior Art Data.   Let us consider as a first example for circularity the case of data annotation in cross-lingual patent retrieval. This task is a subclass of cross-lingual information retrieval and economically extremely relevant. If a company wants to file a patent application, it is important that the new patent cites all previous patents that are relevant to the claim of its originality. The task of identifying relevant patents is called "patent prior art search." In practice, the patent applicant adds all citations that are relevant, to the best of his knowledge, and then this list is refined by patent examiners specifically trained on certain areas of technology. The machine learning task is to aid the patent inventor or patent examiner by automatic prior art search for a set of patent queries over a search repository of foreign-language patents documents.

An established technique to create large datasets for patent prior art search is to determine relevance ranks from different types of patent citations [Graf and Azzopardi, 2008, Guo and Gomes, 2009, Piroi and Tait, 2010]: the most relevant patents are those in the same patent family, indicating the same invention disclosed by common inventors and patented in more than one country (relevance level $r = 3$); very relevant patents are the ones cited in search reports by patent examiners ($r = 2$); and lowest relevant patents are citations added by patent applicants ($r = 1$). These four exclusive conditions build a rule system shown in Table 2.3 that allows deterministically assigning relevance ranks to all query-document pairs.

Large-scale information retrieval datasets such as Yahoo!'s "Learning to Rank" data [Chapelle and Chang, 2011] or Microsoft's LETOR dataset [Qin et al., 2010] contain complex measurements such as BM25 scores [Robertson and Zaragoza, 2009], language model

Table 2.3: Definition of relevance ranks based on patent citation information. Note that the definition is exclusive so that only one condition applies at a time.

Condition	Relevance Score
No citation	0
Inventor citation	1
Examiner citation	2
Family patent	3

scores [Zhai and Lafferty, 2001], or PageRank scores [Brin and Page, 1998] as features. In our cross-lingual patent retrieval experiment, we use two complex features, one consisting of the cosine-similarity of the tf-Idf scores [Jones, 1972] from the Google-translated query and the search document, the other being a neural similarity score derived by training a deep neural network on query and search document text and category data [Kuwa et al., 2020].

The data used in our experiment are a subset of the dataset used by Kuwa et al. [2020] for cross-lingual patent retrieval from Japanese to English. The gold standard relevance ranks were been produced by the deterministic rule system shown in Table 2.3. The data consist of 425,065 observations, including 2,000 patent queries (each with around 250 relevant documents at various levels of relevance) and 200 sampled irrelevant documents per query. For our experiment, the data are split into a training set of 1,500 queries (with 318,375 observations of query-document pairs), and a test set of 500 queries (with 106,690 observations of query-document pairs).

Let us assume the following scenario: a research team wants to use our dataset to train a cross-lingual patent retrieval system without, however, knowing how the gold standard relevance rankings were defined. The goal of the research team is to find out if a deterministic procedure has been used to assign relevance ranks, and to reconstruct the deterministic rule system in an intelligible way, in order to avoid including features on which target labels are deterministically defined into their model. On suspicion that the standard approach of using citation information could have been used to define gold standard relevance rankings, our research team extracts information on patent citations from the raw patent representations and includes them to the set of input features. In order to test the validity of the dataset, the research team applies the circularity test to the powerset of features that can be constructed from the input features in Table 2.4.

Table 2.5 shows the top five models trained during the search procedure. All models that include the citation features inventor, examiner, and family, perfectly reproduce the training data, as shown by values of $D^2 = 100\%$. The model consisting of only these three features, excluding tf-Idf or neural, is the least complex one. Furthermore, as shown in Figure 2.7, the feature shapes of these three features show that they perfectly reconstruct the target function.

Table 2.4: Feature set for cross-lingual patent retrieval

	Feature	Meaning	Range
(1)	`neural`	similarity score learned by neural network	$\mathbb{R}$
(2)	`tf-Idf`	cosine similarity of tf-Idf scores	$\mathbb{R}$
(3)	`inventor`	indicator for inventor citation	$\{0, 1\}$
(4)	`examiner`	indicator for examiner citation	$\{0, 1\}$
(5)	`family`	indicator for family patent	$\{0, 1\}$

Table 2.5: Top five models visited during circularity search for IR training data

Rank	Included Features	D^2	Complexity
1	`{inventor, examiner, family}`	100%	5.00
2	`{inventor, examiner, family, neural}`	100%	6.33
3	`{inventor, examiner, family, tf-Idf}`	100%	7.95
4	`{inventor, examiner, family, neural, tf-Idf}`	100%	11.10
5	`{examiner, family, neural, tf-Idf}`	95%	22.00

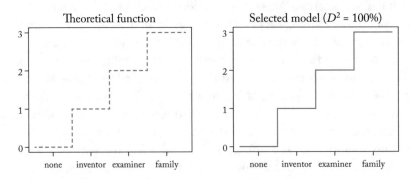

Figure 2.7: Feature shape of citation features reconstructing target labeling function.

This is a first indicator that the set of citation features has been used to deterministically define the target labels, thus revealing them as potentially circular.

Further circularity evidence is obtained by comparing the feature shapes of a model trained on all features to the feature shapes of one where the circularity candidates, i.e., the citation features, were omitted. The left column of Figure 2.8 shows the feature shapes of the tf-Idf and neural features in a model without citation features. The strong contribution of these features

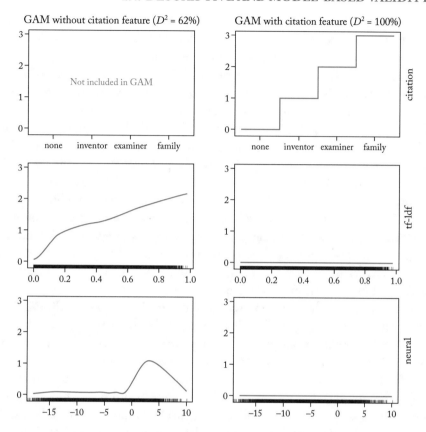

Figure 2.8: Feature shapes of GAM trained with (right column) and without access to citation information (left column), showing nullification of non-circular features in the presence of circular features.

to the prediction of relevance scores is visible with a D^2 value of 62%. For example, the plot on the middle left shows that relevance score is a nearly linear function of tf-Idf score. The top right plot of Figure 2.8 shows the feature shape of the citation features for a model that includes all features. Like any model that includes citation features, this model has a D^2 value of 100%, and it allows us to exactly reconstruct the theoretical step function of relevance scores. However, as seen in the middle and bottom right plots of Figure 2.8, the contribution of the tf-Idf and neural feature in the model that combines all features is completely nullified. We note that this nullification in Figure 2.8 is perfect in that the feature shapes of the nullified features are constant zero lines. This confirms our analysis of the citation features being circular in the investigated patent retrieval dataset.

Circularity in Medical Data.   Another frequent case of circularity in data annotation is the measurement-based determination of gold standard labels in medical data science. A typical task in medical data science is the construction of machine learning based (early) disease diagnosis systems. Let us consider the case of sepsis which is a prevalent (especially among intensive care patients) and lethal disease [Rudd et al., 2020] whose early stages are hard to diagnose. Early diagnosis, however, is crucial to start an effective treatment. Since the introduction of the Sepsis-3 definition [Seymour et al., 2016, Singer et al., 2016], the Sequential Organ Failure Assessment (SOFA) score [Vincent et al., 1996] has played a crucial role in sepsis diagnosis. Together with a suspicion of infection, a defining property of sepsis according to the Sepsis-3 definition is a change in total SOFA score ≥ 2 points consequent to an infection, for SOFA scores defined for six organ systems. The SOFA scores are based on thresholds of clinical measurements. For example, the SOFA scores for the liver and the kidney are based on thresholding measurements of biochemical processes occurring in the respective organ systems. A standard technique to assign gold standard sepsis labels is to use the criteria of suspected infection and two-point increase in SOFA score within a 24-hour period, e.g., in the 2019 PhysioNet Challenge on Early Prediction of Sepsis From Clinical Data [Reyna et al., 2019].

Let us consider the following scenario: our goal is to predict SOFA scores by machine learning. Similar to the PhysioNet Challenge dataset [Reyna et al., 2019], the gold-standard SOFA labels in our data are assigned by applying thresholds on clinical measurements, following the Sepsis-3 definition, to data from 620 intensive care patients from the surgical intensive care unit of the University Medical Centre Mannheim, Germany (see Schamoni et al. [2019] for a detailed description). Let us first consider the liver SOFA score: out of the 45 features used in Schamoni et al. [2019], we consider the clinical measurements of bilirubin (bili), aspartate aminotransferase (asat), quick-inr (quinr), alanin aminotransferase (alat), and cardiac output (hzv) as possible features to describe the liver SOFA score. These features were selected based on the magnitude of their bivariate correlation with the liver SOFA score. As shown in Table 2.6, the deterministic rule to define the SOFA score for the liver is based solely on intervals of bilirubin values. Similar to the data of Reyna et al. [2019], our feature set thus includes the clinical measurements on which SOFA labels, here liver SOFA, are defined. Our goal is to apply a statistical test that exposes this dataset design as circular, although or precisely because it is so common in measurement-based sciences.

Figure 2.9 shows the feature shape of the bilirubin feature for the liver SOFA score for a GAM model with 100 knots that includes solely the bilirubin feature. Unsurprisingly, the GAM model exactly reconstructs the step function defined by bilirubin intervals.

Figure 2.10 shows the feature shapes of two more complex GAMs trained on the liver SOFA data. Both models include the features asat, quinr, alat, and hzv, however, with (right column) and without (left column) access to bilirubin measurements. As any model that includes the bilirubin feature, the model in the right column has a D^2 values of 100%, where the model that includes bilirubin as sole feature has the least degrees of freedom out of all models in the

Table 2.6: Definition of liver SOFA score based on bilirubin levels

Condition	Liver SOFA Score
0 < bilirubin ≤ 1.2	0
1.2 < bilirubin ≤ 1.9	1
1.9 < bilirubin ≤ 5.9	2
5.9 < bilirubin ≤ 11.9	3
bilirubin > 11.9	4

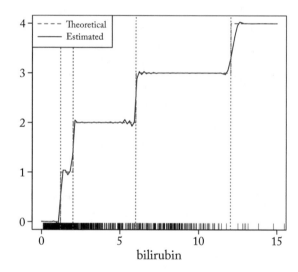

Figure 2.9: Feature shape of bilirubin feature reconstructing the target labeling function.

powerset. As shown in the left column of Figure 2.10, a model trained on the four features asat, quinr, alat, and hzv, excluding bilirubin, explains the data at a D^2 value of 26% and shows nonneglible contributions of these features. However, as soon as the bilirubin feature is added to the model, the contribution of these features is completely nullified, as seen in the last four rows of the right column. We note that even at an enlarged scale, the feature shapes of the nullified features approximate constant zero lines. This allows us to identify bilirubin as a circular feature in the dataset for liver SOFA score.

Things become a bit more complex, but also more interesting, for the kidney SOFA score. The features in this experiment consist of clinical measurements of creatinine (crea), urine output in the previous 24 hours (urine24), pH-value of the arterial blood (artph), blood urea nitrogen (bun), body temperature (temp) and serum lactate (lactate). As shown in Table 2.7, the deterministic rule scheme for the kidney SOFA score is defined as a step function of the kidney status,

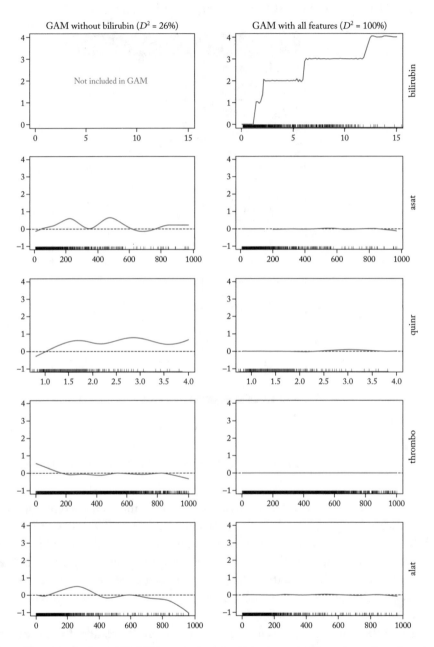

Figure 2.10: Feature shapes of GAM trained with all features (right column) and without access to bilirubin measurement (left column), showing nullification of non-circular features in the presence of circular features.

Table 2.7: Definition of kidney SOFA score based on creatinine and urine levels

Condition 1	Condition 2	Kidney SOFA Score
0 < creatinine ≤ 1.2	500 < urine	0
1.2 < creatinine ≤ 1.9		1
1.9 < creatinine ≤ 3.4		2
3.4 < creatinine ≤ 4.9	200 < urine ≤ 500	3
creatinine > 4.9	0 < urine ≤ 200	4

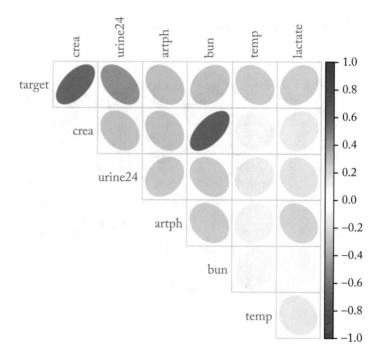

Figure 2.11: Correlation analysis of clinical measurements with kidney SOFA score.

depending on the maximum score of two conditions, based on measurements of creatinine and urine output.

The correlation analysis shown in Figure 2.11 demonstrates that all of the above-defined features are moderately correlated with kidney status. Thus, a distinction between "circular" and simply "strongly correlated" features requires thresholding and is an improper tool to assess invalidity.

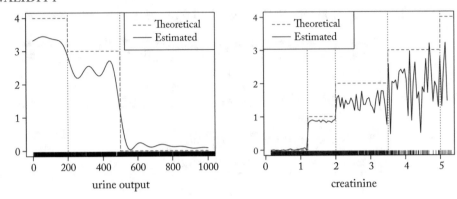

Figure 2.12: **Feature shape of creatinine and urine features reconstructing the target labeling function.**

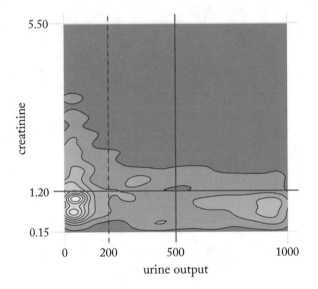

Figure 2.13: **Bivariate distribution of urine and creatinine output in data.**

Training a GAM consisting of the single feature of urine output on the ICU data shows that the feature shape of the urine feature almost exactly models the theoretical step function (Figure 2.12, left plot). The GAM trained with creatinine as the only feature (Figure 2.12, right plot) shows a less perfect fit of the theoretical step function. This is indicated by the empty tassels in the rug plot for the creatinine feature shape. As can be seen by inspecting the bivariate distribution of creatinine and urine in our data in Figure 2.13, most data points with critically high creatinine level also have a critical low urine level, thus the variables are highly confounded.

The reason for the suboptimal fit of the theoretical step function in the case of creatinine is data sparsity in the areas of urine output > 500 and creatinine > 1.2. These are the data areas where a high kidney status would be caused solely by high creatinine levels. However, there are enough data points across the whole range of urine outputs so that a satisfactory fit of the theoretical step function is possible by the feature shape of the urine feature. Still, the highest D^2 value of 95% with the fewest degrees of freedom out of all models is obtained by a model including only creatinine and urine as features, thus serving as a strong indicator for circularity of this feature set.

Figure 2.14 compares the feature shapes of a model using all six features (right column) with the features shapes of a model that excludes the candidate circular features of creatinine and urine (left column). The top two plots in the right column are identical to the feature shapes of urine and creatinine shown in Figure 2.12. The D^2 value of the models on the right reach 95%, compared to 25% for the models without circular features. The bottom four plots show that the contribution of any feature in the model without creatinine and urine (left column) is nullified by inclusion of urine and creatinine as features (right column). We note that even at an enlarged scale, the feature shapes of the nullified features approximate constant zero lines. This again confirms the identification of urine and creatinine as circular features in the dataset for SOFA score.

Circularity in Machine Learning Prediction

A further use case of the circularity test is an analysis of the validity of black-box machine learning models. In this case we do not have access to the training data that were used to optimize the machine learning model. Instead, all we have is model predictions on test data $T = \{(x^m, \hat{y}^m)\}_{m=1}^{M}$. The question we would like to answer is whether we can detect, from the test-set predictions of the black-box model alone, whether the model that performs the predictions relies on features that allow reconstructing a deterministic target functional definition.

Circularity in Machine Learning for Patent Prior-Art Search. Let us consider an example that is inspired by the KISS principle ("keep it simple and straightforward") that has beenapplied in patent prior art search by Magdy and Jones [2010]. The idea of this principle is to automatically obtain the citations of a given query patent in a patent retrieval task, and to improve the search by incorporating this information into the search results. Magdy and Jones [2010] apply this principle in a white-box manner by directly appending IDs of cited patents to the result list of a simpler information retrieval technique such as tf-Idf [Jones, 1972]. We are interested in the scenario where the information retrieval model is a black box, i.e, where we can access the machine learning model only via its predictions on test data. The approach we take is inspired by knowledge distillation where the predictions of a black-box teacher model are used as training data for a GAM student model that is based on all combinations of input features. The circularity test described above is then applied to the GAM with the goal of detecting circular features that define the target label among the candidate input features.

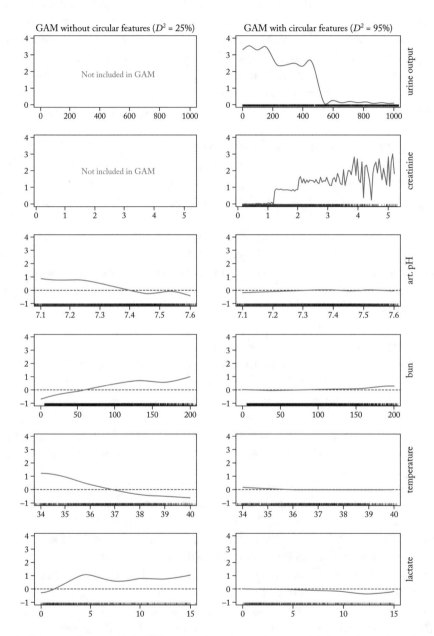

Figure 2.14: Feature shapes of GAM trained with all features (right column) and without access to urine and creatinine measurements (left column), showing nullification of non-circular features in the presence of circular features.

The black-box model used in our experiment computes a nonlinear combination of the scores listed in Table 2.4 using a feedforward neural network (or multi-layer perceptron (MLP)).[13] In our experiment, the target labels are defined as binary relevance ranks for patent queries, and were constructed deterministically by assigning a relevance level of 1 for either inventor citation, examiner citation, or family membership, and a relevance level of 0 for all other documents. The parameters of the teacher neural network are trained for logistic regression on 1,500 queries, resulting in 318,375 observations of query-document pairs. The predictions were thresholded at 0.5 and evaluated with respect to F1 score [Manning et al., 2008]. The teacher neural network on the test set of 500 queries reaches 100% F1. As we will see, this result is too good to be true, since it can be traced back to the teacher neural network reconstructing the deterministic target function while ignoring all other features of the model.

As a first circularity check, we fit a student GAM[14] model that has access to all features in Table 2.4 and treats the neural teacher model's predicted labels similar to gold standard labels. The student model is trained on the 500 test queries that were annotated with relevance ranks predicted by the teacher neural network, resulting in 106,690 query-document observations. Figure 2.15, right column, shows a student model including citation features, reaching a D^2 value of 100%. The three plots in this column show that any model including citation features has learned to rely exclusively on them. A student model that does not include citation features, but only tf-Idf and the neural joint score, is shown in the left column of Figure 2.15. It reaches a respectable D^2 value of 69% and shows a strong contribution of the tf-Idf and neural joint score features to the prediction. However, the step function feature shapes in the left column are completely nullified in the student model in the right column that includes citation features, shown in the flat lined feature shapes in the right column. This confirms that the teacher model must have incorporated the functional definition of relevance ranks via citations as feature into the model.

In order to confirm that our student GAM is not hallucinating circularity, we conducted a control experiment where we trained a teacher neural network explicitly without access to the citation features. As shown in Figure 2.16, the teacher without citation information yields an F1 score of 75.9% on the test set, while the teacher with citation information reaches an F1 score of 100%. Next, we fitted two student GAMs that had access to all features. One GAM was distilled from the teacher trained with citation features, the other GAM was distilled from the teacher trained without citation features. The first GAM is identical to the right column of Figure 2.15 and repeated in the right column of Figure 2.16. We can clearly see that the function represented by the teacher with citation features is identical to the deterministic definition of the target. The student distilled from the teacher without citation access, shown on the left, again

---

[13]The feedforward neural network was implemented in pytorch.org. It consists of 7 layers, with an ascending, then descending number of neurons per layer, and a tanh activation function. It was trained for regression using PyTorch's SGD optimizer, with batch size 64, learning rate .01, without dropout, for 5 epochs. All other optimizer settings are default values of PyTorch's SGD optimizer.

[14]For the binary classification data, we use a GAM that assumes a binomial response variable and a logistic link function.

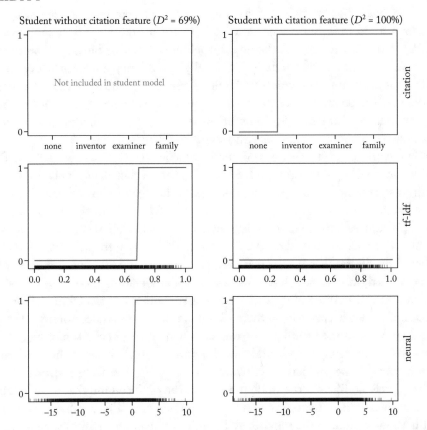

Figure 2.15: Feature shapes of two student GAMs for the same teacher which had access to all features during training. The student in the right column did have access to citation features, while the student in the left column did not. Features in the presence of citation features are nullified.

confirms a strong contribution of the tf-Idf and neural score features to the prediction, however, this contribution is nullified if the teacher has access to citation features.

Furthermore, we performed an ablation study where all citation features were set to zero on the test data. This experiment demonstrates the effect of the citation features on the system performance. We observed a dramatic drop in F1 score for the teacher incorporating citation features, from 100% on the test set including citation features to 0% on the ablation test set not including citation information.

An example of *partial circularity* is given in Figure 2.17. In this example, only information about inventor citations (left column) or information about inventor and examiner citations (right column) is included as features for the teacher model. The inclusion of the first type of

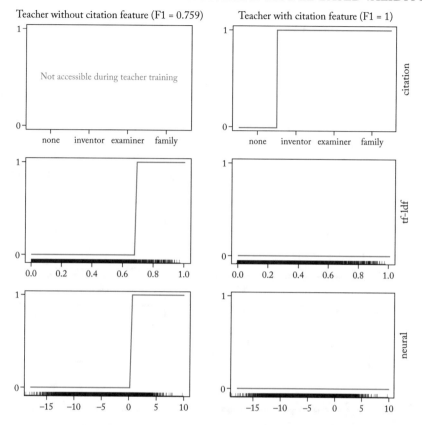

Figure 2.16: Features shapes of two student GAMs that had access to all features, where the teacher in the right column had access to citation features, while the teacher in the left column did not. Features in the presence of citation features are nullified.

information is similar to the effect of bias features which are strongly correlated with the target label, but do not suffice to exactly reconstruct the target function. Information about examiner citations can be seen as an illegitimate feature since relevance judgements obtained from patent examiners are "leaks from the future" [Kaufmann et al., 2011] if patent prior art search is supposed to support the patent examiner. Our analysis shows that a teacher network that has access to inventor and examiner citations reaches an F1-score of nearly 100% on the test set, while a teacher that has access to inventor citations only reaches an F1-score of 83%. The feature shapes of the student GAMs trained on predictions of the respective teacher models clearly identify the use of the respective features during training, shown in the top row of Figure 2.17. For a teacher that uses only inventor citations, the feature shapes of the tf-Idf and neural features of the student GAM still show a strong contribution (second and third row in left column of

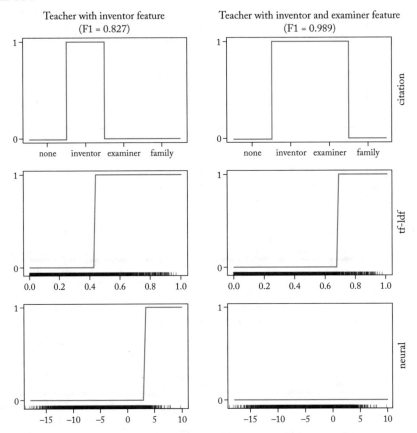

Figure 2.17: Feature shapes of cross-lingual patent retrieval features and partially circular citation features against relevance scores.

Figure 2.17). However, a teacher that uses both inventor and examiner citations diminishes the contribution of the tf-Idf feature, shown by a right-shift of the respective feature shape (second row in right column of Figure 2.17) and nullifies the contribution of the neural score feature (third row in right column of Figure 2.17). Since the functional definition of the target relevance labels has only partially been included in training of the teacher model, the features are only partially nullified in the student GAM.

Circularity in Machine Learning in Medical Data Science.   Let us next consider circularity in the prediction of liver SOFA scores. We want know whether we can tell from the test set predictions alone, without knowing the training data, if a neural network is able to reconstruct the functional definition of liver SOFA scores given in Table 2.6, and whether the learned predictions of the neural network are only applications of this rule. We again employ knowledge

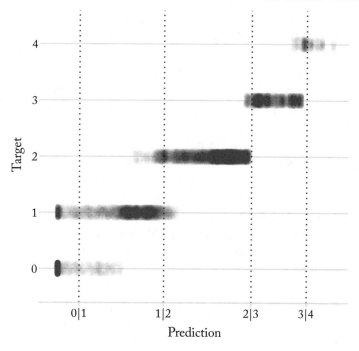

Figure 2.18: Distribution of teacher model score by target class on liver SOFA test set.

distillation: as a teacher network, we consider a feedforward neural network[15] that was trained for regression on 323,404 measurement points of the ICU data for 620 patients described in Schamoni et al. [2019]. Furthermore, thresholds to turn the real-valued teacher network output scores into discrete SOFA scores were learned. The predictions were tested on another 80,671 measurement points. The train and test data include all 45 clinical measurements described in Schamoni et al. [2019] as input features and use liver SOFA scores that were assigned automatically following the functional definition in Table 2.6 as gold standard labels. The accuracy [Manning et al., 2008] of the feedforward teacher network on the test data is 98.1%, where the most accurate predictions were made for the target scores 0, 1, 2, and 3, with minor mispredictions for target class 4 (see Figure 2.18).

Again, this result seems too good to be true, and requires an investigation by a circularity test. Starting from the feature representation of all 45 clinical measurements described in Schamoni et al. [2019], we select the 5 features that are most highly correlated with the label predicted by the teacher model: bilirubin (bili), thrombocytes (thrombo), cardiac output (hzv),

---

[15]The feedforward neural network was implemented in pytorch.org. It consists of 7 layers, with an ascending, then descending number of neurons per layer, and a ReLU activation function [Glorot et al., 2011]. It was trained for regression using PyTorch's SGD optimizer, with batch size 64, learning rate .01, and dropout rate of 0.2 in hidden layers, for 5 epochs. All other optimizer settings are default values of PyTorch's SGD optimizer.

systematic vascular resistance index (svri), and urine output (urine). Based on the predictions of the teacher feedforward network and these five features, we train a GAM student model with 100 knots. As can be seen from Figure 2.19, top right, the objective function of liver SOFA scores can be recreated very accurately by GAM student models including the bilirubin feature with a D^2 value of 99%. Out of all models, the one that includes only bilirubin as feature has the fewest degrees of freedom. The left column shows that all other features have a strong contribution to the prediction if bilirubin is not included in the model, yielding D^2 values of 70%. However, as can be seen in the right column, the contribution of all other features except bilirubin is nullified in any model including bilirubin. To conclude, we identified the bilirubin feature as sufficient to perform a deterministic prediction of the liver SOFA scores assigned by the teacher neural network, while we ruled out other features as deterministic predictors despite their strong correlation with the predicted target labels. We can therefore assume that the neural network that produced the test set predictions included bilirubin as circular feature during training, and it learned nothing but how to reproduce the known deterministic rule to assign liver SOFA scores based on bilirubin levels.

Let us further consider circularity in model prediction for the more complex kidney SOFA score. As a teacher model, we train the feedforward neural network described above[16] for regression on automatically assigned kidney SOFA labels, following the functional definition in Table 2.7. The accuracy of the teacher feedforward network on the test labels is 92.2%, with minor misclassifications happening for target scores 2 and 3 (see Figure 2.20). Out of the 45 input features, we select the 5 features that are most highly correlated with the kidney SOFA score predicted by the teacher model. These are the clinical measurements of creatinine (crea), urine output in the previous 24 hours (urine24), pH-values of arterial blood (artph), blood urea nitrogen (bun), and bilirubin (bili). We train a student GAM with up to 230 knots on the these five features and the labels predicted by the teacher model. As can be seen in the top two plots on the right of Figure 2.21, the theoretical step function can be reasonably approximated in the areas where enough training data points are available. For example, a model trained on the single feature urine output (top right plot in Figure 2.21) appropriately represents the theoretical steps by the function estimate. A sketchier approximation is obtained from a model with creatinine as the only feature (second plot on the right of Figure 2.21). This is due to data sparsity, indicated by the empty tassels in the rug plot. However, the model with the fewest degrees of freedom out of all models and highest D^2 value of 93% is the one that only includes urine and bilirubin as features (right column), whereas models without creatinine and urine (left column) reach a D^2 value of 61%. Furthermore, the contributions of features like bilirubin, bun, or artph, as shown by the feature shapes in the left column, are nullified if creatinine and urine are included in the model, as shown in the third to fifth plot in the right column of Figure 2.21. Again, this confirms that creatinine and urine are circular features that can deterministically predict the target

---

[16]Minor differences in meta-parameter settings to the model trained for liver SOFA prediction include a smaller batch size of 32 and a dropout rate of 0.

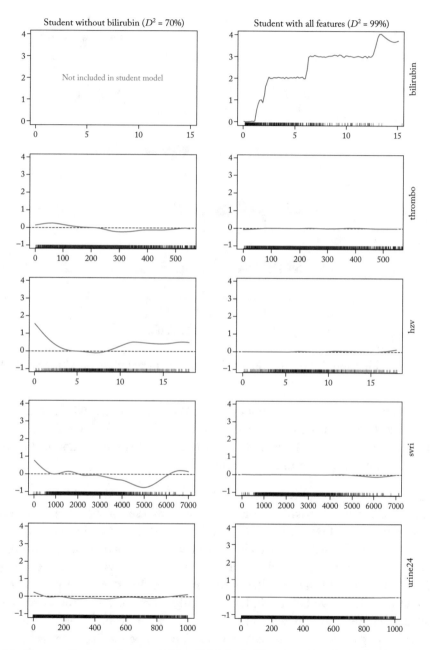

Figure 2.19: Feature shapes of two student GAMs for the same teacher which had access to all features during training. The student in the right column did have access to bilirubin, while the student in the left column did not. Features in the presence of bilirubin features are nullified.

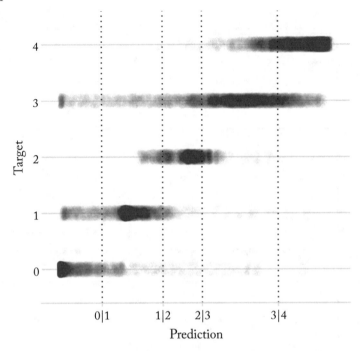

Figure 2.20: Distribution of teacher model score by target class on kidney SOFA test set.

labels assigned by the teacher neural network. We can therefore assume that the teacher neural network must have included creatinine and urine as features during training, and it thus learned nothing besides how to reproduce the known deterministic definition of kidney SOFA scores based on thresholds of creatinine and urine.

Discussion.   The examples discussed in this section use real-world datasets and are based on the building blocks of machine learning algorithms used in benchmark competitions in the fields of cross-lingual patent retrieval [Piroi and Tait, 2010] and medical data science [Reyna et al., 2019]. We showed that an inclusion of measurements that deterministically define target outcomes as input features in the data representation allows machine learning algorithms to reconstruct the functional definition of the target, leading to circular predictions that are based solely on what is known beforehand. Our circularity test is a tool for a clear-cut identification of circular features in machine learning data and black-box models such as neural networks.

Including circular features into a model can happen deliberately or inadvertently. However, in any case they will hinder effectively transferring machine learning expertise to real-world applications in these economically and socially important fields and should clearly be avoided. First, machine learning models trained on data including the defining measurements for target outputs will yield nearly perfect predictions on input data including the defining measurements,

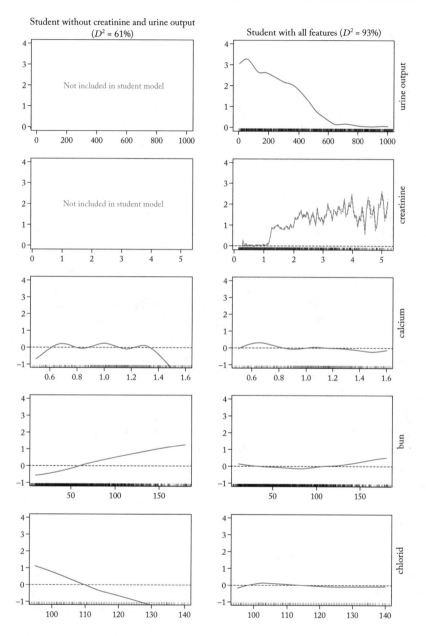

Figure 2.21: Feature shapes of two student GAMs for the same teacher which had access to all features during training. The student in the right column did have access to creatinine and urine features, while the student in the left column did not. Features in the presence of creatinine and urine features are nullified.

but they cannot be transferred to unseen data where the defining features are not or only incompletely available. Second, a circular learning setup that nullifies the contribution of all features except those defining the target dashes the hope to detect features that could shed new light on predictive patterns.

In order to avoid validity problems by circular features, any dataset provider or organizer of a benchmark testing challenge should explicitly disclose the functional definition of target labels if a deterministic rule was used in the dataset creation. Furthermore, participants in the benchmark testing challenge should be warned not to include features that deterministically define the target labels in their models.

Another solution is to rely on implicit expert knowledge in data annotation instead of following automatic data annotation via deterministic functional definitions. Such an approach has been presented by Schamoni et al. [2019] for the area of sepsis prediction. Here the gold standard labels are obtained in the form of an electronic questionnaire which records attending physicians' daily judgements of patients' sepsis status, thus exploiting implicit knowledge of clinical practitioners. As shown in Schamoni et al. [2019], the κ agreement coefficient between expert labels and algorithmically generated Sepsis-3 labels is 0.34, which is to be considered minimal or weak agreement. This shows that even if one could argue that expert decisions are potentially influenced by known sepsis definitions, the circularity issue in this setup is minimal. Machine learning based on such non-circular data then allows detecting potentially surprising findings, such as the identification of increased sepsis risk with higher concentration levels of thrombocytes, contradicting the SOFA-based Sepsis-3 definition, but in accordance with other research on sepsis [de Stoppelaar et al., 2014].

What are further potential cases of circularity beyond those discussed here, or in other words, how likely is it that other datasets and machine learning models exhibit a yet undetected circularity problem? Critical candidates are machine learning applications in empirical sciences like medicine that define the objects of their research, e.g., diseases, by rigid measurement procedures. We conjecture that any disease prediction task in medical data science needs to be extra cautious to keep measurements that define target outcomes separate from data representations for machine learning. The same is true for any other prediction task based on data derived from measurements.

In sum, promising results for machine learning prediction may well be achieved even in circular setups, however, cautious analyses are required in order to discern whether the machine learning prediction is based on an accurate estimate of the known functional definition from data—something which could have been achieved easier by a programmatic application of the deterministic thresholding function—or whether the actual strength of machine learning has been exploited—namely to learn predictions based on patterns in data that go beyond known deterministic rules.

2.5   NOTES ON PRACTICAL USAGE

The techniques presented in this chapter lend themselves to two basic use cases. First, the validity of a given dataset might be in question. We discussed bias features (Section 2.1.1), illegitimate features (Section 2.1.2), and circular features (Section 2.1.3) as possible causes for invalidating a dataset. We presented statistical tests in form of the Dataset Bias Test (Definition 2.2), Transformation Invariance Test (Definition 2.3), and Circularity Test (Definition 2.6) to identify these types of features.

Second, the validity of the predictions of a black-box machine learning model might be in question. The same statistical validity tests that can be applied to gold standard data can also be applied to datasets of features and labels predicted by machine learning models, mimicking a knowledge distillation setup.

The recommended action to take upon detection of a validity problem is clear in case of illegitimate and circular features: such features should be discarded from the data representations since they prevent meaningful machine learning beyond the reconstruction of information that is either standardly unavailable (in case of illegitimate information) or already known (in case of circular information). Machine learning approaches like regularization that foster generalization are not remedies against circular or illegitimate features, but they simply conceal such problems by preventing overfitting on the dataset whose validity is in question. In contrast, bias features are an evasive concept since they are on essential to most tasks, but still undesired. This makes the prevention of bias a machine learning problem by itself that goes beyond the scope of this book.

CHAPTER 3

Reliability

Reliability is closely intertwined with validity. On the one hand, reliability is a necessary, but not a sufficient, condition for validity. On the other hand, in the pursuit of high reliability, validity tends to get lost, for example, by oversimplifying measurement procedures or by overly strict annotation instructions. More often than not, the notion of reliability is claimed as the primary criterion for the adequacy of a measurement. However, the concept of reliability is not clearly defined for predictions in NLP and data science. There are a multitude of metrics that are commonly applied to measure reliability in data annotation, and a different set of measures that address reliability of model predictions. The goal of this chapter is to provide a clear definition of reliability that applies to data annotation and model prediction alike, and that can be operationalized into a procedure to assess reliability of data annotation and model prediction in concrete applications in NLP and data science.

3.1   UNTANGLING TERMINOLOGY: RELIABILITY, AGREEMENT, AND OTHERS

Krippendorff [2004] states the *measurement theory conception of reliability* as follows:

> A research procedure is **reliable** when it responds to the same phenomena in the same way regardless of the circumstances of its implementation.

The terminological confusion starts as soon as the terms "research procedure" and "circumstances of its implementation" are given a concrete interpretation. Krippendorff himself is interested in measuring reliability of data annotations for a fixed sample of data points by a fixed selection of human coders—the "research procedure"—given their different response styles or different exposition environments—the "circumstances of their implementation." Another interpretation that will be of interest in this chapter is to replace the "research procedure" by a machine learning model, and the "circumstances of the implementation" as variability due to architectural choices or meta-parameter settings in model optimization.

Reliability of measurements of nominal outcomes is frequently called *agreement*, unlike reliability of measurements with continuous outcomes [Hallgren, 2012, Shoukri, 2011], and it is often reserved for the case of human raters representing the research procedure whose reliability is in question. However, given the general measurement theoretic definition above, the concepts of *intra-rater agreement* (the consistency of annotation results of a human rater on repeated trials on same data) can be seen as parallel to *test-retest reliability* (the correlation between results of the same test on two occasions under otherwise identical circumstances). The concept of *inter-rater agreement* (the consistency of annotation results of two or more human raters on the same data) can be seen as parallel to forms of *test-test reliability* in measurement theory (the correlation between results of equivalent forms of tests performed under otherwise identical circumstances).

To add to the confusion, Krippendorff [2004] uses the term *stability* to denote intra-rater agreement, and he gives inter-rater agreement the name *reproducibility*. A further term called *replicability* is introduced by Dror et al. [2017] to denote consistency over different datasets from different domains or languages. To complete the confusion, Plesser [2018] lists different interpretations of the terms *replicability* and *reproducibility*, and adds the term *repeatability* that brings the variable of different researchers into the mix. Finally, Goodman et al. [2016] clarify things a bit by making explicit the aspect of reproducibility by distinguishing *methods reproducibility*, *results reproducibility*, and *inferential reproducibility*.

In the following, we will stick to the term *reliability* and provide an operational definition that applies to data annotation and model prediction processes in NLP and data science alike. For this purpose, we rely on a unified conceptualization of data annotation and model prediction as measurement procedures.

3.2   PERFORMANCE EVALUATION AS MEASUREMENT

Similar to validity, reliability is standardly considered as a property of measurements. The key concern of a reliability study is to estimate the consistency of measurement scores across replicated measurements. In Chapter 2, we conceptualized a measurement as the determination of a function value for a homomorphic mapping of empirical structures into a numerical system, and we looked at predictions in NLP and data science as instances of measurements. Furthermore, we characterized predictions by the functional relation of input features in a p-dimensional feature vector $\mathbf{x} = (x_1, x_2, \ldots, x_p)$ to labels y in a dataset $D = \{(\mathbf{x}^n, y^n)\}_{n=1}^{N}$. While in Chapter 2 the actual systems that performed the predictions were considered fixed and deterministic, here we are interested explicitly in the possible sources of variation after replicated predictions. In the case of data annotation, possible sources of variation include human annotators, repeated annotations by the same annotator, or the test sentences themselves. In the case of machine learning prediction, possible sources of variation include meta-parameters of the machine learning models and properties of test data like the lengths of test sentences. We will denote these *meta-features* by $\mathbf{m} = (m_1, m_2, \ldots, m_q)$. A further difference to the formalization in Chapter 2 is that in most applications we will work with response signals in form of a *performance evaluation score e* of a predicted output $\hat{y}$ under some evaluation metric, instead of with the outputs directly. While in case of regression problems such as the SOFA score prediction discussed in the previous chapter, outputs can be used directly as response signals, this is not possible for NLP applications where outputs are structured labels. However, replacing labels by corresponding evaluation scores allows us to measure reliability for structured prediction problems. For example, in the case of data annotation in interactive machine translation, possible performance evaluation metrics are post-editing time or human translation edit rate [Snover et al., 2006]. In the case of machine learning predictions, for example in machine translation, possible performance evaluation metrics are BLEU [Papineni et al., 2002] or TER [Snover et al., 2006]. Furthermore, note that investigating sources of variation caused by properties of the test data requires the performance evaluation scores to be decomposable over test outputs. We will see different cases of evaluation scores e in the experimental examples discussed below.

The problem of the reliability of a prediction can now be refined as the question of how consistent the relationship between meta-features $\mathbf{m}$ and performance scores e is under replicated performance measurements. Since every configuration of meta-parameters and data is characterized by a distinct representation $\mathbf{m}$, we can consider the relation of each pair $\mathbf{m}, e$ as a function. Furthermore, we can collect a dataset $D = \{\mathbf{m}^l, e^l\}_{l=1}^L$ of $L = M \times N$ performance evaluations for models trained under M meta-parameter configurations and evaluated on N test data points. These data can then be used as training data in the model-based approach presented in Section 3.3.3.

3.3   DESCRIPTIVE AND MODEL-BASED RELIABILITY TESTS

Before diving into the details of model-based reliability testing, we will discuss common descriptive statistics that have been proposed as reliability metrics. The most well-known such metrics are agreement coefficients such as Scott's π [Scott, 1955], Cohen's κ [Cohen, 1960], or Krippendorff's α [Krippendorff, 2004] that are commonly used to measure reliability in data annotation processes in NLP and data science. Furthermore, we will look at applications of common randomization-based techniques like the bootstrap [Efron and Tibshirani, 1993] to develop estimates of reliability of model prediction processes.

3.3.1   AGREEMENT COEFFICIENTS FOR DATA ANNOTATION

Krippendorff's α coefficient is a widely used agreement measure in NLP, at least since the survey paper of Artstein and Poesio [2008]. Its attractiveness is due to the fact that it is based on the simple concept of percent agreement that is adjusted to include agreement by chance, similar to Scott's π [Scott, 1955] or Cohen's κ [Cohen, 1960], but it is applicable to multiple raters and to all standard scales of measurements (nominal, ordinal, interval, and ratio variables). The measure is also easily computable from experimental data by collecting relative count statistics instead of optimizing a machine learning model. This convenience is due to a fixed choice of a model for computing chance agreement, done by sampling without replacement from marginal distributions averaged over raters. As we will see, this model assigns maximum randomness to chance agreement, a counter-intuitive principle that leads to unmotivated radical changes in value, and even makes the agreement coefficient undefined if no variation in measurement is encountered.

Let us consider the computation of α for two raters and nominal predictions, using an example from Krippendorff [2004] for binary ratings of two raters A and B on 10 items:

	1	2	3	4	5	6	7	8	9	10
A	1	1	0	0	0	0	0	0	0	0
B	0	1	1	0	0	1	0	1	0	0

In order to compute the α coefficient, we first need to sum up the number of observed rating values in a matrix of two raters, while omitting references to the individual raters. The entries of this matrix are called observed coincidences o_{ck}:

	0	1				0	1	
0	o_{00}	o_{01}	n_0		0	10	4	14
1	o_{10}	o_{11}	n_1		1	4	2	6
	n_0	n_1	n			14	6	20

Second, in order to represent what could happen by chance, we need to calculate expected coincidences e_{ck}. These are calculated by randomly sampling without replacement from the marginals, averaged across raters. This random sampling process can be illustrated by the following simple urn model. Assume we write each rating of the two raters on a ball and put it in an urn. Then we draw two balls from the urn without replacing the first one. For our example, expected coincidences are computed as follows:

	0	1				0	1	
0	e_{00}	e_{01}	n_0		0	9.6	4.4	14
1	e_{10}	e_{11}	n_1		1	4.4	1.6	6
	n_0	n_1	n			14	6	20

The expected coincidence e_{00} of chance agreement between raters A and B on two 0s is calculated by letting the first rater draw a 0 in 14 out of 20 cases, and letting the second rater draw a 0 in $14 - 1$ out of $20 - 1$ cases. By multiplying these two probabilities by the total number of 20, we get the expected frequency of 9.6 pairs of two 0s. The remaining expected coincidences are computed accordingly, as shown below:

$$e_{00} = \frac{n_0}{n} \cdot \frac{n_0 - 1}{n - 1} \cdot n = \frac{14}{20} \cdot \frac{13}{19} \cdot 20 = 9.6$$

$$e_{11} = \frac{n_1}{n} \cdot \frac{n_1 - 1}{n - 1} \cdot n = \frac{6}{20} \cdot \frac{5}{19} \cdot 20 = 1.6$$

$$e_{01} = \frac{n_0}{n} \cdot \frac{n_1}{n - 1} \cdot n = \frac{14}{20} \cdot \frac{6}{19} \cdot 20 = 4.4$$

$$e_{10} = \frac{n_1}{n} \cdot \frac{n_0}{n - 1} \cdot n = e_{01}$$

From these coincidence tables, the α coefficient is computed as follows:

$$\alpha = \frac{\text{observed agreement - chance agreement}}{n - \text{chance agreement}}$$

$$= 1 - \frac{\text{observed disagreement}}{\text{expected disagreement}}$$

$$= 1 - \frac{o_{01} + o_{10}}{e_{01} + e_{10}}$$

$$= 1 - \frac{o_{01}}{e_{01}}.$$

For the example above, this yields $\alpha = 1 - \frac{4}{4.421} = 0.095$. The idea of α as a measure of chance-corrected agreement is motivated by the values at the end of the range. That is, an α value of 0, indicating the absence of reliability, is obtained in the case where observed and expected disagreement are matters of pure chance and thus equal. An α value of 1, indicating perfect reliability, is obtained in the case where there is no observed disagreement. In our example, α is relatively low at barely 10%, while the uncorrected observed agreement—the percent of cases of agreement out of all analyzed cases—is at 60%. The explanation for this discrepancy lies in the fact that the assumed model of chance agreement attributes 56% of agreement to chance, as can be seen by calculating $(9.6/20) + (1.6/20) = 56\%$.

Note that the definition of α given above does not guarantee $\alpha \in [0, 1]$. For example, α will be negative for the following table of ratings:

	1	2	3	4	5	6	7	8
A	0	0	0	0	0	0	1	0
B	0	0	0	0	0	0	0	1

First, we note that uncorrected percent agreement is at $6/8 = 75\%$. The matrices of observed and expected coincidences are as follows:

	0	1	
0	12	2	14
1	2	0	2
	14	2	16

	0	1	
0	12.13	1.87	14
1	1.87	0.13	2
	14	2	16

The calculation of expected disagreement is again based on the value $e_{01} = e_{10}$:

$$e_{00} = (14/16)((14-1)/(16-1))16 = 12.13$$
$$e_{11} = (2/16)((2-1)/(16-1))16 = 0.13$$
$$e_{01} = (14/16)(2/(16-1))16 = 1.87$$

We note that the α value is negative since $\alpha = 1 - \frac{2}{1.87} = -0.07$. The explanation lies again in the computation of chance agreement which amounts to $(12.13/16) + (0.13/16) = 76.6\%$. This means that all of the observed agreement (75%), and more, is attributed to chance.

Unfortunately, even if one agrees with the principle of maximum randomness, the stipulation of chance agreement by a random sampling model has further ramifications. While values of α at the ends of the range were supposed to motivate the measure, extreme values can also be obtained by nonsensical abnormalities, defeating a clear interpretation of the measure. Consider the following table of binary ratings of two raters A and B on our 10 items:

	1	2	3	4	5	6	7	8
A	0	0	0	0	0	0	0	1
B	0	0	0	0	0	0	0	1

The uncorrected percent agreement amounts to 100%, and α reaches a maximum due to no observed disagreement: $\alpha = 1 - \frac{0}{e_{01}} = 1$. If this result is desired, consider a tiny change in the table that throws a wrench in the works:

	1	2	3	4	5	6	7	8
A	0	0	0	0	0	0	0	0
B	0	0	0	0	0	0	0	1

A change of one rating by one rater renders observed and expected coincidences equal:

	0	1	
0	14	1	15
1	1	0	1
	15	1	16

$$e_{00} = (15/16)((15-1)/(16-1))16 = 14$$
$$e_{11} = (1/16)((1-1)/(16-1))16 = 0$$
$$e_{01} = (15/16)(1/(16-1))16 = 1$$

This yields $\alpha = 1 - \frac{1}{1} = 0$, although the uncorrected percent agreement is still at $7/8 = 88\%$. Consider another tiny change in the table, yielding zero variation:

	1	2	3	4	5	6	7	8
A	0	0	0	0	0	0	0	0
B	0	0	0	0	0	0	0	0

Now $\alpha = 1 - \frac{0}{0}$ is technically undefined. Nevertheless, Krippendorff [2004] arbitrarily defines it to be 0 in this case, while the uncorrected percent agreement is 100%.

Discussion. To summarize, chance-corrected agreement measures like Scott's π, Cohen's κ, or Krippendorff's α can be written in the following form:

$$\frac{\text{observed agreement - chance agreement}}{n - \text{chance agreement}}.$$

All measures stipulate a hypothetical model for chance agreement, where the central differences lie in choices such as sampling with replacement (Scott's π and Cohen's κ) or without replacement (Krippendorff's α) from distributions for individual raters (Cohen's κ) or for the observed ratings averaged over raters (Scott's π and Krippendorff's α).

A crucial similarity between the measures is the fact that the above described counter-intuitive principle of maximum randomness, and the resulting abnormalities, apply to all chance-corrected agreement metrics in a similar way.[1] Furthermore, all listed shortcomings apply to all scales.

Arguably, the main shortcoming common to π, κ, and α is the fact that these measures are descriptive statistics that do not permit to draw conclusions that generalize beyond concrete raters and concrete data points examined in a concrete experiment. That is, agreement measures do not allow explaining the reason for high or low agreement by general properties of raters or data, or by interactions between raters and data. However, a useful reliability measure should provide the possibility to understand lacking agreement in terms of properties of raters and data.

3.3.2 BOOTSTRAP CONFIDENCE INTERVALS FOR MODEL EVALUATION

Inference beyond concrete prediction experiments is indispensable if reliability of model prediction is to be measured. In contrast to data annotation, the interest is not in the reliability of human annotations which are used to generate a fixed and static dataset, but in the reliability of predictions of a machine learning model that is supposed to be used over and over, not just in the one experiment in question. Thus, even if the interval scaled variant of Krippendorff's α would,

---

[1]See Zhao et al. [2013] for an exhaustive list of paradoxes and abnormalities of chance-corrected agreements measures like π, κ, and α.

in principle, be applicable to measure reliability of model prediction processes, it does not make sense to estimate a single number indicating the reliability of a machine learning prediction for a given set of tested meta-parameters, without generalizing across the concrete meta-parameter settings and data that were used in a particular experiment.

In the machine learning community, the problem of reliability of model prediction has been addressed by computing confidence intervals for performance evaluation metrics computed on test data. In the following, we will take a closer look at the approaches of Henderson et al. [2018] and Lucic et al. [2018] who propose bootstrap-inspired resampling procedures to compute confidence bounds for evaluation scores on test data. The approach advocated in Lucic et al. [2018] aims to capture the variability of an evaluation metric introduced by a random search over meta-parameters during training by calculating a confidence interval for the expected maximum performance under a computational budget. Henderson et al. [2018] use bootstrap confidence intervals to compare the performance differences due to different meta-parameter choices in a reinforcement learning setting. The details of the implemented algorithms to construct bootstrap confidence sets vary from study to study. In the following, we will briefly summarize the central concepts of confidence intervals and bootstrap techniques, and sketch an algorithm to apply these ideas to construct confidence intervals for evaluation metrics under a computational budget.

The concept of a confidence interval can be defined following Shao [2003] as follows.

Definition 3.1 (Confidence Interval). Let $\mathcal{P}$ denote a family of distributions and $\theta \in \mathbb{R}$ be an unknown parameter of $P \in \mathcal{P}$. Further, let $\alpha \in (0, 1)$ and $Y = (Y_1, Y_2, Y_3, \ldots, Y_n)$ be a random sample generated from the random process described by $\mathcal{P}$. Then the estimated interval $[\hat{\theta}_l(Y), \hat{\theta}_u(Y)]$ is called a *confidence interval for θ at confidence level* $1 - \alpha$ if $\forall P \in \mathcal{P}$ holds

$$P(\hat{\theta}_l(Y) \leq \theta \leq \hat{\theta}_u(Y)) \geq 1 - \alpha. \tag{3.1}$$

Formally, a confidence interval is a function of the randomly sampled data Y from which estimators of the lower bound $\hat{\theta}_l(Y)$ and the upper bound $\hat{\theta}_u(Y)$ need to be constructed. This construction needs to be done in a way such that the true parameter θ is covered by the interval by a fraction of at least $(1 - \alpha)$ of all possible samples. The most prominent example of a confidence interval is the case of independent and identically distributed Gaussian data with unknown mean. For this case, the bound estimators can be constructed analytically, yielding the well-known formula for a 95% confidence interval of the population mean μ, where $\bar{x}$ is the sample mean and $\sigma_{\bar{x}}$ denotes the standard error:

$$\bar{x} - 1.96\sigma_{\bar{x}} \leq \mu \leq \bar{x} + 1.96\sigma_{\bar{x}}. \tag{3.2}$$

This can be interpreted by a statement that at a 95% confidence level, 95% of intervals constructed in the same way on numerous samples will cover the population mean μ within an interval that is $2 \times 1.96 = 3.92$ standard error units wide, centered around the sample mean.[2]

In the case that the family $\mathcal{P}$ can not be specified for an application, confidence intervals can be constructed via nonparametric[3] bootstrap sampling distributions. A simple approach is the so called *standard method*, which constructs bootstrapped confidence intervals by plugging bootstrap estimates of $\sigma_{\bar{x}}$ into Equation (3.2).[4]

A use case of special interest to the machine learning community is the calculation of confidence intervals for the maximum out-of-sample performance of an evaluation metric under a given computational budget. The variation that is to be quantified in these applications is variance due to meta-parameter configurations in model training that significantly impacts the maximum performance achievable on a given test set. Let p_m denote a model trained under a meta-parameter configuration m, where M is the size of all meta-parameter configurations, and $B \leq M$ is the computational *budget* that restricts the number of meta-parameter search trials. Inspired by the ideas presented in Dodge et al. [2019], Henderson et al. [2018], Lucic et al. [2018], and Tang et al. [2020], a somewhat unconventional bootstrap-like procedure can be defined by resampling performance evaluation scores in order to compute a confidence interval for an evaluation metric under a computational budget[5]:

Algorithm 3.2 (Confidence Interval for Evaluation Metric under Computational Budget)

1. Generate M meta-parameter configurations for considered model class.

2. For each $m = 1, \ldots, M$: train model p_m and calculate the performance evaluation score $u_m = u(p_m)$.

---

[2]A realized confidence interval must not be interpreted in a probabilistic fashion: once a sample is drawn and the confidence bounds are determined, the resulting interval either includes θ or not, but all involved quantities are non-random: $\hat{\theta}_l(Y)$ and $\hat{\theta}_u(Y)$ have been observed, and θ is an unknown, but non-random quantity. The $(1 - \alpha)$ probability relates to the confidence of the estimation procedure, not to a specific calculated interval.

[3]The main principle of the nonparametric bootstrap is the substitution of the unknown data distribution by the empirical distribution obtained from the i.i.d data sample. Generating data from this distribution is equivalent to drawing with replacement from the original sample. This method is especially effective for large sample sizes.

[4]A method to construct a bootstrap confidence interval with better coverage of the true parameter is the so-called percentile method [Cohen, 1995, Efron and Tibshirani, 1993]. In general, the construction of bootstrap confidence intervals is a somewhat delicate problem for which no general conclusive method has been found yet. Improved methods and an illustrative discussion of this topic are presented in Efron and Hastie [2016].

[5]Obviously, in this setup the probability to sample the best performing model p_m^* is non-decreasing with B. Furthermore, note that the following algorithm might give an improper picture if the meta-parameter space is unbounded. A proper choice of B is thus a non-trivial problem.

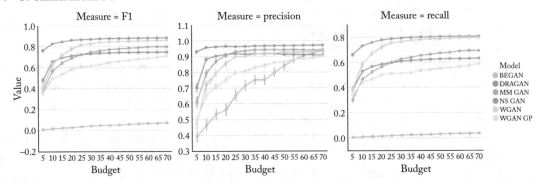

Figure 3.1: Mean and 95% confidence intervals for F1-score, precision, and recall of GANs for different computational budgets. Graphics from Lucic et al. [2018].

3. For each $B \leq M$: construct a bootstrap distribution by K times drawing B random samples with replacement from $\{u_m : m = 1, \ldots, M\}$. For each sample select the maximum performance score.

4. Calculate the mean and the standard deviation of this distribution. In order to construct a confidence interval plug both estimates into Equation (3.2).

The use of confidence interval for measuring reliability of model prediction performance is two-fold: first, the confidence interval can be used to directly signify *error bars* that visualize the confidence bounds on the mean value in a plot. For example, Figure 3.1 shows the mean values as dots and 95% confidence intervals as vertical bars for the means of the evaluation metrics F1-score, precision, and recall for computational budgets (number of visited meta-parameter configurations) to train meta-parameter variants of Generative Adversarial Networks (GANs) [Lucic et al., 2018]. Confidence bounds can then be used to assess the reliability of an evaluation under different meta-parameter settings. The rationale is that at the same level of confidence, smaller confidence bounds indicate higher reliability, thus the maximum performance score obtained by the meta-parameter search is more likely to be repeatable.

Second, a bootstrap confidence interval can be used to perform a *conservative significance test*[6] by comparing confidence intervals. Given two mean evaluation scores of two competing systems and the confidence intervals about these means, one can prove that if the confidence

---

[6]Conservative significance tests are characterized by the fact that the true probability of incorrectly rejecting the null hypothesis is never greater than the nominal significance level, i.e., the test has a low Type I error, but also low power. More information on statistical significance testing is found in Chapter 4 of this book.

intervals do not overlap—the upper bound of one is below the lower bound of the other—then the means will be significantly different [DeGroot and Schervish, 2012].

Discussion.   Bootstrap techniques are popular in NLP and data science since they can be applied to compute confidence intervals for complicated nonlinear evaluation metrics such as F1-score [Manning et al., 2008], BLEU [Papineni et al., 2002], or ROUGE [Lin and Hovy, 2003], used for classification, machine translation, or summarization, respectively. The often cited reason for the flexibility of the bootstrap is the fact that it does not make any assumptions about the underlying population distribution except that the original sample is representative of the population [Cohen, 1995]. However, in order to guarantee correctness of a bootstrap confidence interval, a normality assumption on the sampling distribution of the evaluation metric has to be made, or else the evaluation metric u has satisfy the condition of the existence of a monotone transformation $\hat{\phi} = g(u)$ such that the sampling distribution of $\hat{\phi}$ is normal. Efron and Tibshirani [1993] list a few normalizing transformations whose existence guarantee correctness of the bootstrap confidence interval, in the sense that the confidence bounds are the same when applying the bootstrap technique to the test statistic before and after transformation. The existence of such correcting transformations is usually not considered when applying bootstrap techniques to complex test statistics.

Another potential problem of bootstrap techniques is a potential failure of bootstrap consistency [Canty et al., 2006]. This can happen if the test set from which bootstrap samples are drawn is not representative of the population, leading to a poor approximation of the cumulative population distribution. Another possible reason for inconsistency of the bootstrap is a situation where the parameter to be estimated is on the boundary of the parameter space [Andrews, 2000, Bickel and Freedman, 1981]. This happens in bootstrap-inspired and related resampling procedures that compute expected maximum performance under a given budget [Dodge et al., 2019, Lucic et al., 2018], since the true parameter will be poorly covered by the constructed confidence interval of the expected maximum.

An alternative to bootstrap methods is the use of cross-validation techniques to compute confidence bounds on expected performance evaluation scores, taking into account the variability in data samples. For example, Dietterich [1998] proposes five iterations of two-fold cross-validation, while Nadeau and Bengio [1999] propose cross-validation runs on several half-splits of the data separately, in order to obtain conservative estimates of the standard error to be used to construct standard confidence bounds. These methods can become quite computation intensive since they involve several runs of training and evaluation on the obtained data splits. Furthermore, as shown by Bengio and Grandvalet [2004], there is no unbiased estimator for the variance of cross-validation because of correlations among the evaluation scores for each data split. This can lead to underestimates of variance which in turn leads to narrow standard confidence intervals with coverage below the nominal desired level. Only recently Bates et al. [2021] introduced a nested cross-validation scheme to estimate standard errors more accurately, leading to confidence intervals with approximately correct coverage.

Lastly, and most importantly, neither expected maximum evaluation scores nor error bars based on confidence intervals tell us what we wish to know most urgently when reliability of model prediction is in question, namely the reasons for lacking reliability. What a modeler wants to obtain from a reliability analysis is a hint at which meta-parameters have the most influence on variations in evaluation scores, and how meta-parameter settings interact with properties of test data. In order to answer these questions, model-based approaches to reliability, as described in the next section, are needed.

3.3.3   MODEL-BASED RELIABILITY TESTING

In classical psychological measurement theory [Lord and Novick, 1968], an undifferentiated measurement error accompanies every experimental measurement. More recent work in psycho-metrics liberates classical theory by employing variance component analysis to untangle multiple sources of variation that contribute to the variability in measurement [Brennan, 2001]. For performance evaluation in data annotation, variance decomposition means decomposing the total variance into factors corresponding to measurement conditions such as raters, sentences, or interactions between raters and sentences. The same idea can be transferred to performance evaluation in model prediction. Here one could select as factors of variability measurement conditions such as meta-parameter settings of machine learning models, properties of test sentences, or interactions between these factors.

In the following, we will introduce the central concepts of variance component analysis [Searle et al., 1992], and adapt these ideas to the fields of NLP and data science. We will take a model-based approach to estimate variance components, based on random effects of linear mixed effects models (LMEMs) [McCulloch and Searle, 2001]. Our main goal will be to use variance components to define a reliability coefficient that assesses the reliability of data annotation or model prediction performance by the amount of variance that is attributable to objects of measurement in relation to total variance.

Variance Component Analysis

Let us consider performance evaluation in interactive machine translation as an example for reliability studies [Bentivogli et al., 2016, Green et al., 2014, Karimova et al., 2018, Kreutzer et al., 2020, Simianer et al., 2016]. The response variable Y_{sr} in such an experiment is an evaluation score measuring human annotation effort, e.g., human Translation Edit Rate [Snover et al., 2006]. A *tautological decomposition* shows that it can be modeled as consisting of four components:

$$Y_{sr} = \mu + (\mu_s - \mu) + (\mu_r - \mu) + (Y_{sr} - \mu_s - \mu_r + \mu). \tag{3.3}$$

The components are the grand mean μ of the observed evaluation score across all raters r and sentences s; the deviation $(\mu_r - \mu)$ of the mean for each individual rater μ_r from the grand mean μ; the deviation $(\mu_s - \mu)$ of the mean for each sentence μ_s from the grand mean μ;

and the residual error, reflecting the deviation of the observed score Y_{sr} from what would be expected given the first three terms. Except for μ, each of the components of the observed score varies from one rater to another, from one sentence to another, and from one rater-sentence combination to another. Since these components are uncorrelated with each other, the total variance $\sigma^2(Y_{sr} - \mu)$ can be decomposed into the following *variance components*:

$$\sigma^2(Y_{sr} - \mu) = \sigma_s^2 + \sigma_r^2 + \sigma_{residual}^2, \tag{3.4}$$

where σ_s^2 and σ_r^2 denote the variance due to sentences and raters, and $\sigma_{residual}^2$ denotes the residual variance component including the variance due to interaction of s and r.

In the psychometric approach to reliability of Brennan [2001], the conditions of measurement that contribute to variance in the measurement besides the objects of interest are called *facets* of measurement. In the example above, the objects of interest in our measurement procedure are the sentences. They are the essential conditions of measurement. The only facet of measurement in this example are the raters, while the objects of interest are not usually called a facet. An experiment using this so-called one-facet fully crossed design would randomly select a finite subset of sentences and raters and observe the scores for all possible combinations. Multi-facet designs allows modeling interaction effects explicitly. For example, adding a facet for instantiations i of repeated annotations by the same raters on the same sentences would lead to the following two-facet fully crossed design:

$$
\begin{aligned}
Y_{sri} = {} & \mu + (\mu_s - \mu) + (\mu_r - \mu) + (\mu_i - \mu) \\
& + (\mu_{sr} - \mu_s - \mu_r + \mu) \\
& + (\mu_{si} - \mu_s - \mu_i + \mu) \\
& + (\mu_{ri} - \mu_r - \mu_i + \mu) \\
& + (Y_{sri} - \mu_{sr} - \mu_{si} - \mu_{ri} + \mu_r + \mu_s + \mu_i - \mu),
\end{aligned}
\tag{3.5}
$$

and the following variance components:

$$\sigma^2(Y_{sri} - \mu) = \sigma_s^2 + \sigma_r^2 + \sigma_i^2 + \sigma_{sr}^2 + \sigma_{si}^2 + \sigma_{ri}^2 + \sigma_{residual}^2. \tag{3.6}$$

The facets of measurement in this design include raters r, instantiations i, and facets for interactions sr, si, and ri, with objects of measurements being sentences s.

Estimation of the variance components has traditionally been done by so-called ANOVA estimators consisting of expected mean square equations. These date back to Fisher [1925] and are discussed extensively in Brennan [2001]. A more flexible alternative is to model variance components as random effects in LMEMs, as will be described in the next section.

Linear Mixed Effects Models

In the notation presented in Appendix A.2, for a given dataset of N input-output pairs $\{(x^n, y^n)\}_{n=1}^N$, the general form of an LMEM is as follows:

$$\mathbf{Y} = \mathbf{X}\boldsymbol{\beta} + \mathbf{Z}\mathbf{b} + \boldsymbol{\epsilon}, \tag{3.7}$$

where $\mathbf{X}$ and $\mathbf{Z}$ are known design matrices that relate a vector of fixed effects $\boldsymbol{\beta}$, a random effects vector $\mathbf{b}$, and an N-dimensional vector of residual errors $\boldsymbol{\epsilon}$ to N stacked response variables $\mathbf{Y}$. While fixed effects can be observed exhaustively and are modeled as parameters of a standard linear model, random effects are modeled as normally distributed random variables, and corresponding observations are treated as random samples from a larger population. Similar to the random error, random effects have a normal distribution with zero means

$$\mathbf{b} \sim \mathcal{N}(0, \boldsymbol{\psi_\theta}), \tag{3.8}$$
$$\boldsymbol{\epsilon} \sim \mathcal{N}(0, \boldsymbol{\Lambda_\theta}), \tag{3.9}$$

where $\boldsymbol{\psi_\theta}$ and $\boldsymbol{\Lambda_\theta}$ are variance-covariance matrices parameterized by $\boldsymbol{\theta}$.

How do the variance components or facets described above relate to LMEMs? Following Jiang [2018], each component $\nu_f = \mu_f - \mu$ denoting a deviation from the mean for a facet f, is simply modeled as a component of the *random effects* vector $\mathbf{b}$, and each corresponding variance component σ_f^2 is modeled as an entry of the diagonal variance-covariance matrix $\boldsymbol{\psi_\theta}$. In the notation of Section 3.2, the facets encoded in the random effects vector correspond to components of the meta-feature vector $\mathbf{m}$, and response variables Y correspond to the evaluation scores e, yielding a performance evaluation dataset $D = \{\mathbf{m}^l, e^l\}_{l=1}^{L}$ of $L = M \times N$ performance evaluations for M meta-parameter configurations evaluated on N test data points, to train an LMEM. In the following, we will simplify the notation by omitting subscripts for facets when specifying response variables Y, and we will denote all facet-specific deviations by ν_f.

One of the advantages of using LMEMs to estimate variance components is that the same model structure can be used for nested experimental designs, i.e., for designs that are special cases of the fully crossed design.[7] The price for this flexibility is that although LMEMs look like a linear model, the linear combination of fixed effect predictor variables and normally distributed random components yields a nonlinear objective function with an elaborate estimation methodology. Crucially, while fixed effect parameters are optimized directly, random effects are predicted from a normal distribution whose variance-covariance matrix is estimated. This leads to the possibility of using LMEMs without any fixed effects to directly estimate random effects with the sole purpose of variance decomposition in reliability studies. We will use such random-effects-only LMEMs extensively in our experiments. For details on modeling and parameter estimation for LMEMs we refer the reader to Appendix A.2 and to further literature [Demidenko, 2013, McCulloch and Searle, 2001, Pinheiro and Bates, 2000, West et al., 2007, Wood, 2017].

---

[7]In the world of ANOVA, differences in design such as each measurement object being rated by a different set of raters instead of by all raters meant that a one-way instead of a two-way ANOVA estimator had to be used, while in LMEM estimation this results in a missing data situation that is handled well by explicit estimation of the random effects variance-covariance matrix. A discussion of further experimental designs is beyond the scope of this book. We refer the reader to Brennan [2001] for various nested designs useful in reliability studies, and to McGraw and Wong [1996] and Shrout and Fleiss [1979] for earlier work on the same topic. Other advantages of LMEMs over ANOVA estimators include the ability to handle multiple random effects, each with its own variance matrix or with its own random slope. See Baayen et al. [2008], Barr et al. [2013] and Bates et al. [2015] for further discussions on the advantages of LMEMs over mixed-model ANOVA estimators.

Reliability Coefficients

The final ingredient of a model-based approach to reliability is the definition of a coefficient that relates variance components to each other, instead of inspecting them in isolation. The key concept is the so-called *intra-class correlation coefficient (ICC)*, dating back to Fisher [1925]. A fundamental interpretation of the ICC is as a measure of the proportion of variance that is attributable to the objects of measurement. The name of the coefficient is derived from the goal of measuring how strongly objects in the same class are grouped together in a measurement. The coefficient is computed as the ratio of the variance between objects of interest σ_B^2 to the total variance σ_{total}^2. The latter includes variance within objects of interest σ_W^2, or simply undifferentiated residual variance σ_ϵ^2:

$$ICC = \frac{\sigma_B^2}{\sigma_{total}^2} = \frac{\sigma_B^2}{\sigma_B^2 + \sigma_W^2} = \frac{\sigma_B^2}{\sigma_B^2 + \sigma_\epsilon^2}. \tag{3.10}$$

In our example of data annotation in interactive machine translation, the objects of measurement are test sentences. An annotation can be considered reliable if most of the variance is explained by variance between sentences and not by variance within a sentence, such as variance caused by inconsistencies of human annotators or by residual variance due to unspecified facets of the measurement procedure. That is, variance between objects of measurement, here sentences, is considered substantial variance and should outweigh all other nonsubstantial variance.

In order to quantify the components σ_B^2 and $\sigma_W^2 = \sigma_\epsilon^2$, we compute the variance due to the objects of interest and decompose the undifferentiated residual error into variance components for various facets. The key idea of Brennan's [2001] approach is to first estimate variance components from initial experimental observations and then to use these estimates to find an optimal measurement procedure for final use.[8]

Let us consider the two-facet fully crossed design with the objects of interest being sentences s, and measurement facets for rater r and instantiation i. Furthermore, let n_r denote the number of raters, and n_i the number of instantiations. Brennan [2001] interprets total variance as the variance between objects of interest, here σ_s^2, plus the absolute error variance σ_Δ^2 that includes variance components for all facets and interactions, except σ_s^2:

$$\sigma_\Delta^2 = \frac{\sigma_r^2}{n_r} + \frac{\sigma_i^2}{n_i} + \frac{\sigma_{sr}^2}{n_r} + \frac{\sigma_{si}^2}{n_i} + \frac{\sigma_{ri}^2}{n_r n_i} + \frac{\sigma_{residual}^2}{n_r n_i}. \tag{3.11}$$

---

[8]Brennan [2001] calls the first a generalization study (or G-study) associated with an universe of admissible observations, and the second a decision study (or D-study) associated with a universe of generalization. We will not use this terminology in order to avoid confusion with the use of the terms "generalization" and "decision" in machine learning.

Brennan [2001] then defines an absolute reliability coefficient Φ[9] that relates the variance between objects of interest σ_s^2 to the total variance:

$$\Phi = \frac{\sigma_s^2}{\sigma_s^2 + \sigma_\Delta^2}. \tag{3.12}$$

Our notion of reliability coefficient will be a generalized version of an absolute reliability coefficient, denoted by φ. It includes variance components for all random effects of a model except σ_s^2 in the error variance term σ_Δ^2, however the coefficient is more flexible since it does not require to include interaction effects for all facets.

Definition 3.3 (Reliability Coefficient).   Assume facets $f_1, f_2, \ldots$ and selected interactions $s f_1, s f_2, f_1 f_2, \ldots$, with sample sizes $n_{f_1}, n_{f_2}, \ldots$. Then the reliability coefficient φ is computed by the ratio of substantial variance σ_s^2 to the total variance, i.e., to itself and the error variance σ_Δ^2:

$$\varphi = \frac{\sigma_s^2}{\sigma_s^2 + \sigma_\Delta^2},$$

where

$$\sigma_\Delta^2 = \frac{\sigma_{f_1}^2}{n_{f_1}} + \frac{\sigma_{f_2}^2}{n_{f_2}} + \ldots + \frac{\sigma_{s f_1}^2}{n_{f_1}} + \frac{\sigma_{s f_2}^2}{n_{f_2}} + \ldots + \frac{\sigma_{f_1 f_2}^2}{n_{f_1} n_{f_2}} + \ldots + \frac{\sigma_{residual}^2}{n_{f_1} n_{f_2} \ldots}.$$

In the following, we will illustrate the reliability coefficient on examples from data annotation and model prediction. In the first case, objects of measurement are sentences to be annotated, and measurement scores indicate human annotation effort. Facets of measurement are human raters, and repeated instantiations of measurement of the same sentence by the same annotator. In the second case, objects of measurement are test sentences to be translated, and measurement scores are automatic evaluation metrics of model outputs against gold standard references. Facets of measurement are meta-parameters of machine translation models, properties of test sentences, and interactions between these factors. A further example for the second

---

[9]Brennan [2001] calls this coefficient the "index of dependability." We will not use this naming in the following. He also introduces a relative reliability coefficient that is based on a relative error variance $\sigma_\delta^2 = \frac{\sigma_{sr}^2}{n_r} + \frac{\sigma_{si}^2}{n_i} + \frac{\sigma_{residual}^2}{n_r n_i}$ that only sums up variance components interacting with the items of interest. Brennan [2001] denotes this coefficient by $\mathbb{E}\rho^2$ and gives it the name of a "generalizability coefficient." The relative reliability coefficient focuses on the stability of the relative ordering of objects of interest, while the absolute reliability coefficient focuses on the homogeneity of absolute performance score for objects of interest across measurement instances, independent of performance scores for other objects of interest. In the experiments presented in this chapter we will focus on the absolute reliability coefficient.

case is model prediction of SOFA scores where objects of measurement consist of clinical measurements taken in a time series, and measurement scores consist directly of the scores predicted by the model.

Based on these examples and the reliability coefficient specified in Definition 3.3, we can give an operational definition of the concept of reliability as follows:

Definition 3.4 (Reliability).   A performance evaluation of a prediction in data annotation or machine learning is reliable across replicated measurements if the amount of substantial variance outweighs the total error variance at a sufficient ratio.

Clearly, Definition 3.4 relies on the variance components of an LMEM that has been fitted to particular dataset $D = \{\mathbf{m}^l, e^l\}_{l=1}^{L}$ of performance evaluations, and it leaves a set of decisions open to the user. One is, for example, the choice of the threshold above which the ratio is considered to be sufficient. A threshold of 80% is used, for example, by Jiang [2018] as a criterion to determine the reliability of a measurement according the reliability coefficient. Koo and Li [2016] discuss the interpretation of values below and above this threshold.

Reliability of Data Annotation Performance

In applications of this coefficient to measure reliability, it is reasonable to start from a fully crossed initial experiment design for given facets, compute estimates for the variance components, and then conduct a hypothetical study to extend the design by varying the sample sizes for facets until a satisfactory coefficient value is obtained.

Let us use the experiments on interactive machine translation by Kreutzer et al. [2020] for an exemplary study of reliability of data annotation performance. The goal of this study was to improve the performance of a pre-trained neural machine translation system by using human translation quality judgments as supervision signals in fine-tuning. They investigated two modes of human feedback. In the first mode, called "Marking," human raters mark erroneous words in the machine translation output by using an annotation interface to highlight them. In the second mode, termed "Post Edit," human raters correct translations by deleting, inserting, and replacing words or parts of words. For reasons of efficiency and cost, the data annotation for the subsequent fine-tuning process was designed such that every document was annotated by a different user, and no user saw the same document twice. However, for each annotation mode, a set of example sentences was held out to measure reliability of data annotation. That is, for each mode, each of five sentences was annotated three times by each of ten human raters. We will study the reliability of user feedback on these data.

Table 3.1: Variance components in translation marking experiment

Variance Component v	Variance σ_v^2	Percent
sentence s	0.00304	12
rater r	0.00358	14.2
instantiation i	0	0
interaction sr	0.00407	16.1
interaction si	0.00000000000434	0
interaction ri	0	0
residual	0.0145	57.6

A first impression of the reliability of data annotation performance in interactive machine translation can be given by inspecting Figure 3.2. We see that sentences consistently receive a higher quality score for "Post Edit" annotations than for "Marking" annotations. We also see that the assigned scores vary more for "Post Edit" than for "Marking" annotations. Let us now conduct a model-based reliability study for these data. The experiment design is a two-facet, fully crossed design with a variance component for the objects of measurement, i.e., sentences s, and facets for raters r, instantiations i, and interactions sr, si, and ri. The response variable Y that is measured is a reduction of markings and post-edits to sentence-wise quality judgments that compute the ratio of marked or edited words per sentence, respectively [Kreutzer et al., 2020]. This yields the following model

$$Y = \mu + v_s + v_r + v_i + v_{sr} + v_{si} + v_{ri} + \epsilon_{residual}, \qquad (3.13)$$

where μ is the grand mean. Each facet f is associated with a factor $v_f = \mu_f - \mu$ that indicates the deviation of its mean from the related grand mean and is estimated by encoding variance components as random effects of an LMEM.

The estimates of variance components for annotations in "Marking" mode can be seen in Table 3.1. The result corresponds to a computation of the coefficient φ and shows that only 12% of the variance in this experiment can be explained by variance σ_s^2 between objects of measurement. Thus, 88% is attributed to arbitrary particularities of the measurement. Obviously, there is no systematic difference between replicated measurements (the effects containing the instantiation facet have variance components equal to zero). We also see that a large fraction $\sigma_r^2 = 14.2\%$ of measurement variation can be attributed to different marking styles of raters, but this style differences are not uniform across sentences, as seen by $\sigma_{rs}^2 = 16.1\%$. Thus, a large amount of non-attributable variance $\sigma_{residual}^2 = 57.6\%$ remains.

The variance component analysis for the "Post Edit" mode yields the results shown in Table 3.2. A computation of φ shows that by far the largest portion of variance can be attributed to differences in our object of measurement since $\sigma_s^2 = 60.4\%$. We also see that the non-

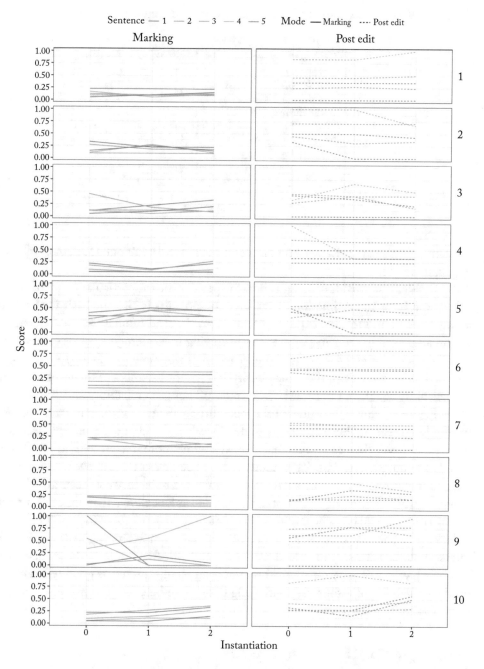

Figure 3.2: Sentence-wise quality judgment score computed as ratio of marked or edited words per sentence, for three rating instantiations of five sentences by each of ten raters.

Table 3.2: Variance components in translation post-editing experiment

Variance Component v	Variance σ_v^2	Percent
sentence s	0.0479	60.4
rater r	0.00138	1.7
instantiation i	0	0
interaction sr	0.0187	23.7
interaction si	0	0
interaction ri	0.000622	0.8
residual	0.0106	13.4

substantial fraction of variance is mostly composed of two components, namely $\sigma_{sr}^2 = 23.7\%$ and $\sigma_{residual}^2 = 13.4\%$.

Besides just providing insights into the peculiarities of particular facets of a measurement, a decomposition and estimation of variance components is also the basis for exploratory studies on efficient and reliable experimental designs. Instead of analyzing a concrete experiment, we are interested in reducing variance by averaging measurements across several raters and instantiations. Concretely, we reduce the variation attributable to a facet f by averaging over n_f repeated measurements of the same object for different instances of the facet. We then compute the reliability coefficient to find the best trade-off between reliability and efficiency.

Figure 3.3 shows the values of the reliability coefficient for measurements of sentence-wise quality judgments of human ratings under "Marking" and "Post Edit" modes, averaged over $n_i = 1, .., 5$ instantiations and plotted against a number of raters $n_r = 1, .., 12$. This study shows that data annotation in "Post Edit" mode yields a coefficient value above 60% for observations of single annotation instances by single raters, while the reliability coefficient in "Marking" mode is only at 12%. Averaging over instantiations and raters shows that about two raters and two instantiations would be sufficient to reach coefficient values of about 80% in "Post Edit" mode. In "Marking" mode, however, averaging measurements from 3–5 rating instantiations from 10–12 raters would be necessary to exceed the 80% threshold. According to the guidelines of Koo and Li [2016], values of φ between 75% and 90% can be interpreted as good reliability. Depending on the availability of resources, a satisfying design can be chosen to maximize reliability under given feasibility restrictions.

Reliability of Model Prediction Performance

Model evaluations in the train-dev-test paradigm usually report a single high score of a model that has been trained with the largest budget, both in terms of maximal hardware resources and maximal computational resources for extensive meta-parameter search (see Dodge et al.

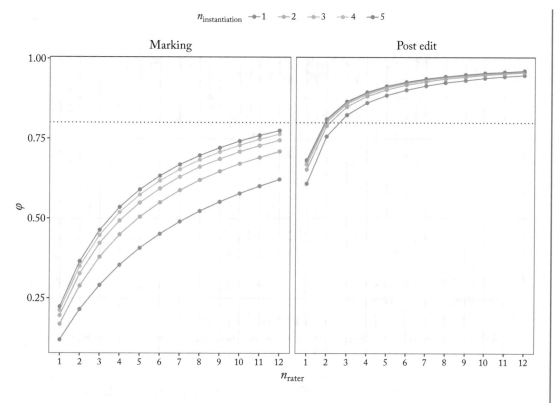

Figure 3.3: Reliability coefficient φ for data annotation performance in "Marking" or "Post Edit" mode, generalized to 5 rating instantiations and 12 raters.

[2019], Henderson et al. [2018], Lucic et al. [2018], Strubell et al. [2019], and Tang et al. [2020] for a discussion). Such evaluation procedures are insufficient for drawing conclusions about the general performance of models, since they do not allow reproducing model predictions if repeated under differing meta-parameter settings. Fortunately, the random effects capabilities of LMEMs allow us to estimate the variance induced by particular meta-parameter settings of machine learning models in a general way, across instantiations of all other meta-parameters. Such a variance component analysis will be useful to assess the importance of meta-parameters, based on their contribution to overall variance, and to assess the reliability of a performance evaluation process, based on the ratio of substantial variance to total variance, including variance due to meta-parameter settings.

Variance Component Analysis of Meta-Parameter Importance.   An established use-case of variance component analysis in the context of meta-parameter search is the use of ANOVA-type techniques to assess the importance of meta-parameters [Hutter et al., 2014, Zimmer et

Table 3.3: Meta-parameters values used in training neural models for prediction of liver SOFA score

Meta-Parameter	Grid Values					
batch_size	1	4	8	16	32	64
dropout	0	0.05	0.1	0.15	0.2	
epochs	1	5	10			
hidden_number	3	5	7			
hidden_size_max	16	32	64	128	256	
learning_rate	0.001	0.01	0.1			
random_seed	−7712	6483	20777			

al., 2020]. We show how variance component analysis based on the random effects of an LMEM can be used for this purpose.

As an example, let us consider a multi-layer perceptron (MLP) that predicts the liver SOFA score and is evaluated by a summative performance metric, such as mean accuracy over the test data instances. The neural model architecture is the same as used in Section 2.4.3 as a teacher model for predicting SOFA scores. The architecture is a feedforward neural network with an ascending, then descending number of neurons per layer, and a ReLU activation function [Glorot et al., 2011]. It was trained for regression using pyTorch's SGD optimizer on 323,404 measurement points of the ICU data for 620 patients described in Schamoni et al. [2019], and evaluated on a test set of another 80,671 measurement points. For each of the 7 types of meta-parameters of the neural network, 3–6 reasonable values were chosen, and a grid of models over all combinations of chosen values for each meta-parameter was trained and evaluated. The meta-parameters include architectural parameters for feedforward neural networks [Rumelhart et al., 1986]: maximal number of neurons in hidden layer (hidden_size_max), number of hidden layers (hidden_number), values of initial learning rate (learning_rate), number of training examples in each gradient computation (batch_size), seed of random number generator (random_seed), number of iterations over training set (epochs), and probability of zeroing out hidden connections during training (dropout) [Srivastava et al., 2014]. Table 3.3 shows the meta-parameter values used in training and evaluation, yielding a fully crossed configuration space of $6 \times 5 \times 3 \times 3 \times 5 \times 3 \times 3 = 12{,}150$ models.

In order to assess the variance contribution of each meta-parameter, we train an LMEM on data points $D = \{\mathbf{m}^l, e^l\}_{l=1}^{L}$, consisting of M meta-features vectors $\mathbf{m}$, each corresponding to a specific meta-parameter configuration of a model, and mean accuracy evaluation scores e obtained by evaluating a model trained under a specific meta-parameter setting on the full test set. Thus, the number of performance evaluation data points in this experiment is $L = M$. The

Table 3.4: Variance components from meta-parameter grid search for neural model prediction of liver SOFA score

Variance Component v	Variance σ_v^2	Percent
residual	0.0000314	61.2
hidden_number	0.0000159	31.0
learning_rate	0.00000318	6.2
batch_size	0.000000517	1.01
hidden_size_max	0.000000260	0.505
dropout	0.0000000599	0.117
random_seed	0.00000000405	0.00788

response variable Y in this experiment is the mean evaluation score e, and each meta-parameter is modeled as random effect $v_{meta-parameter}$ of a random-effects-only LMEM. We a consider model with single random effects without interactions of the following form:

$$Y = \mu + v_{hidden\_size\_max}$$

$$+ v_{hidden\_number}$$
$$+ v_{learning\_rate}$$
$$+ v_{batch\_size}$$
$$+ v_{random\_seed}$$
$$+ v_{epochs}$$
$$+ v_{dropout}$$
$$+ \epsilon_{residual}.$$

$$(3.14)$$

Figure 3.4 shows means and standard deviations of the evaluation score on the test set for each meta-parameter setting. The interpretation of each random effect as a variance component is given in Table 3.4.

We see that the meta-parameter that induces most of the variance in model evaluation is the number of hidden layers, amounting to 31% of the total variance, followed with a wide margin by the learning rate, responsible for 6.2% of the total variance. All other meta-parameters introduce a negligible variance of 1% or less into the performance evaluation of the neural model. This result matches the findings of Zimmer et al. [2020], who also observe the number of layers and the learning rate to be the two most "important" meta-parameters of multilayer perceptrons, even though they were evaluated for different applications with different techniques.

Reliability Coefficients for Meta-Parameter Grid Search.   A usage of variance component analysis that goes beyond a mere assessment of meta-parameter importance is a reliability assessment of model predictions under varying meta-parameter settings. For this purpose, LMEMs

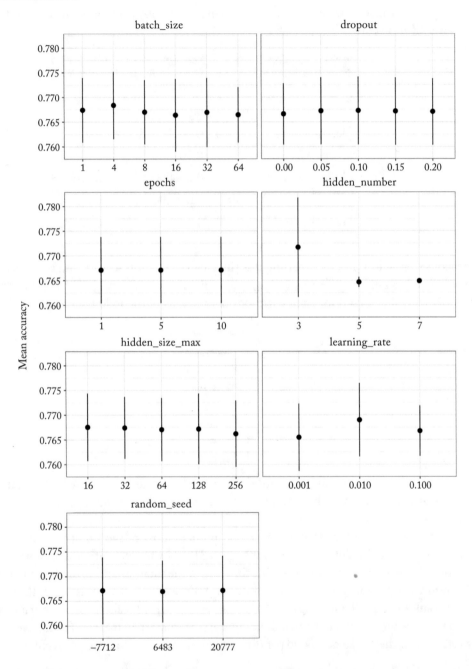

Figure 3.4: Means and standard deviations of mean test set accuracy of neural models trained for prediction of liver SOFA score.

can be trained on data consisting of performance evaluation scores measured separately for items of interest. Based on the variance components of the trained LMEM, a reliability coefficient can be computed that relates variance attributable to items of interest to variance due to meta-parameter variation.

A question naturally arises regarding the feasibility of variance component analysis for large configuration spaces of meta-parameters. As we will see, the standard practice of a meta-parameter search over an incomplete configuration space, either guided by the experience of the modeler (see, for example, Jiang et al. [2019]), or by random search over the configuration space (as suggested by Bergstra and Bengio [2012]), can provide useful data to compute reliability coefficients. Furthermore, a simple check of substantial variance can be performed that assesses only the contribution of the objects of measurement to the total variance. A prerequisite to such a substantial variance check is the assumption of a partially crossed experimental design where selected meta-parameter settings are evaluated against the full set of measurement items. This leads to orthogonal effect estimators for substantial variance components which guarantee that the substantial variance of objects of measurement will stay constant even if the residual variance is further decomposed.

Let us formalize these requirements in the framework of variance component analysis of Searle et al. [1992]. In this framework, independent variables that we called (meta-)features or facets are interpreted as classifications of data, called *factors*, and the individual classes are termed *levels* of a factor. The extent to which different levels of a factor affect the dependent variable is called the *effect* of a level of a factor on the response. *Effect estimators* are, for example, maximum likelihood estimates for random effect parameters of LMEMs. Our interest is in effect estimators for variance components σ_s^2 for substantial factors that stay constant for a given experiment, irrespective of how fine-grained the residual variance is decomposed. This goal can be achieved by choosing an appropriate experimental design that crosses substantial factors with factors corresponding to meta-parameters, according to the following definition.

Definition 3.5   (Crossed and Balanced Design).   A factor is called crossed iff all its levels are observed with all combinations of at least one level all other factors in the experiment. An experimental design is called partially crossed iff at least one factor is crossed, and fully crossed iff all factors are crossed. An experimental design is called balanced iff the number of observations is the same for all factor combinations realized in an experiment.

The special instance of Definition 3.5 that we are interested in is the case of a partial grid search over meta-parameters where each configuration of meta-parameter values is evaluated once for all items of interest, yielding a partially crossed and balanced design. For such a design, we can obtain unique and constant effect estimators for substantial variance components σ_s^2, as expressed in the following proposition.

Proposition 3.6   (Orthogonal Effect Estimator).   *Crossed factors in (fully or partially) crossed and balanced designs are uncorrelated to other factors, and the effect estimators for variance components* *corresponding to these factors are unique, irrespective of the variance decomposition of the residual variance. Such factors and the corresponding effect estimators are called orthogonal.*

Proof sketch. Assume that X is a crossed factor in a partially crossed balanced design with N samples observed in each cell. Without loss of generality, let us denote its levels l^X by $1, 2, \ldots, L_X$ and call $\bar{x} = \frac{1}{L_X}(1 + 2 + \cdots + L_X)$ the level mean. Let Y be another factor considered in the experiment with levels $1, 2, \ldots, L_Y$ and analogously defined level mean $\bar{y}$. In order to show that X and Y are uncorrelated, we have to show that $\sum_{l=1}^{L_X} \sum_{i=1}^{N} (l_{li}^X - \overline{l^X})(l_{li}^Y - \overline{l^Y}) = 0$. The fact that the design is balanced allows us to replace the data means $\overline{l^X}$ and $\overline{l^Y}$ by the corresponding level means $\bar{x}$ and $\bar{y}$. Together with the fact that X is crossed with Y, we obtain the result of zero co-variance:

$$\sum_{l=1}^{L_X} \sum_{i=1}^{N} (l_{li}^X - \overline{l^X})(l_{li}^Y - \overline{l^Y})$$

$$= N \sum_{x=1}^{L_X} \sum_{y=1}^{L_Y} (x - \bar{x})(y - \bar{y})$$

$$= N \sum_{x=1}^{L_X} (x - \bar{x}) \sum_{y=1}^{L_Y} (y - \bar{y})$$

$$= 0.$$

Effect estimators for orthogonal factors are estimated independent of all other factors, thus they can be determined uniquely and stay constant irrespective of the presence or absence of other factors in the total variance decomposition. This holds for ANOVA sum-of-square estimators as well as for maximum likelihood estimators for LMEMs (see Searle et al. [1992], Chapter 4). □

Proposition 3.6 allows us to perform a simple check of the proportion of variance attributable to the objects of measurement, without having to conduct a full variance decomposition. As a first example, let us apply this check to the multi-layer perceptron for the prediction of liver SOFA. The neural model in this example is the same as used in Section 2.4.3 as teacher model for predicting SOFA scores, and as used in the previous section to showcase the computation of meta-parameter importance. While the data for the variance component analysis in the previous section consisted of the summative evaluation metric of mean accuracy over the full test set, evaluated for 12,150 models, the data required to compute the reliability coefficient φ need to consist of a model score for each item of measurement. In this experiment, the items of measurement consist of 80,671 data points of clinical measurements that were collected for 620 patients. Since SOFA score prediction is a regression problem, we can directly use model predictions for each of these measurement points, computed over a small grid of $3 \times 3 \times 3 = 27$ models for each of three values of the meta-parameters learning rate, hidden number, and random seed. For a substantial variance check, we can train the following simple model where response variables Y

Table 3.5: Variance components for substantial variance check of partial meta-parameter grid search for circular neural net for liver SOFA prediction

Variance Component v	Variance σ_v^2	Percent
substantial factor s	0.766	98.5
residual	0.0113	1.46

Table 3.6: Variance components for substantial variance check of partial meta-parameter grid search for non-circular neural net for liver SOFA prediction

Variance Component v	Variance σ_v^2	Percent
substantial factor s	0.162	70.5
residual	0.0663	28.8

consist of clinical measurements and substantial factors s consist of identifiers for measurement points:

$$Y = \mu + v_s + \epsilon_{residual}. \tag{3.15}$$

A substantial variance check for this simple model amounts to computing the ratio of substantial variance σ_s^2 to itself and the undifferentiated residual variance $\sigma_{residual}^2$, corresponding to the reliability coefficient $\varphi = \frac{\sigma_s^2}{\sigma_s^2 + \sigma_{residual}^2}$. As shown in Table 3.5, for the circular model (including bilirubin measurements defining liver SOFA), we obtain a reliability coefficient of 98.5%. This is an excellent example for how an invalid prediction can be highly reliable since the inclusion of circular features allows consistent and accurate predictions even for non-optimal meta-parameter settings. Removing the label-defining feature in Table 3.6 yields a still considerable coefficient value of 70.5% for a substantial variance check. According to the guidelines of Koo and Li [2016], this coefficient value tells us that the variations in the predictions of the neural SOFA score model can be attributed to test data heterogeneity with moderate reliability. A further variance decomposition shows that non-substantial variance is incurred for variations of the meta-parameters of learning rate (0.39%), random seed (0.302%), and hidden number (0.0451%).

Let us next consider the experiments on interactive machine translation by Kreutzer et al. [2020]. The ultimate goal of this study was to use sentences annotated with human markings and post-edits as training data to improve the fine-tuning step of a neural machine translation system. The measurement process in this case consists of evaluating predictions of the neural machine translation system that has been fine-tuned on the correct parts of marked or post-edited

Table 3.7: Meta-parameters values used in basic fine-tuning experiment of neural machine translation model on human marking data in Kreutzer et al. [2020]. Values in **bold face** are used in an extended grid search.

Meta-Parameter	Grid Values			
learning_rate	0.0001	0.0003	0.0005	**0.003**
random_seed	42	43	44	
encoder_dropout	**0**	0.2	0.4	0.6
decoder_dropout	**0**	0.2	0.4	**0.6**
decoder_dropout_hidden	**0**	0.2	0.4	0.6

sentences. The objects of interest thus consist of 1,043 test sentences[10] for which the TER evaluation score [Snover et al., 2006] has been measured against reference translations. The models used in Kreutzer et al. [2020] are encoder-decoder recurrent neural networks (RNNs) with attention [Bahdanau et al., 2015, Luong et al., 2015], 4 bi-directional encoder and 4 decoder layers with 1,024 units each, and embedding layers of size 512. These models are considerably larger than the MLP described above to predict SOFA scores, and they are pre-trained on datasets of over 6 million parallel sentences, and fine-tuned on another 1,042 sentences.

The items of interest in this experiment are the sentences in the test data. Let us apply a substantial variance check to performance evaluation data of a neural machine translation model fine-tuned on sentences annotated in "Marking" mode. These neural model include the following meta-parameters: values of initial learning rate (`learning_rate`), seed of random number generator (`random_seed`), probability of zeroing out hidden connections during training of encoder (`encoder_dropout`), decoder (`decoder_dropout`), and hidden layers of the decoder (`decoder_dropout_hidden`). Ranges of meta-parameter values are shown in Table 3.7. In the original experiment of Kreutzer et al. [2020], a partial grid of 27 models was trained and evaluated. For a substantial variance check, we can train the simple model (3.15) for response variables Y consisting of sentence-level TER scores, and substantial factors corresponding to test sentences s. As shown in Table 3.8, we see that the substantial variance for these experimental data amounts to 82.1% of the total variance.

For a further decomposition of variance due to meta-parameters, we model each meta-parameter as single random effect without interactions and train a random-effects-only LMEM

---

[10]Note that two of the 1,043 test sentences reported in Kreutzer et al. [2020] were duplicates that we removed in our LMEM experiments.

Table 3.8: Variance components for substantial variance check of partial meta-parameter grid search for basic fine-tuning experiment of neural machine translation model on human marking data in Kreutzer et al. [2020]

Variance Component v	Variance σ_v^2	Percent
sentence s	0.0905	82.1
residual	0.0197	17.9

of the following form:

$$Y = \mu + v_s$$
$$+ v_{learning\_rate}$$
$$+ v_{random\_seed}$$
$$+ v_{encoder\_dropout}$$
$$+ v_{decoder\_dropout}$$
$$+ v_{decoder\_dropout\_hidden}$$
$$+ \epsilon_{residual}.$$

(3.16)

An interpretation of each random effect as a variance component is shown in Table 3.9. We see that the meta-parameter which induces the largest variance is the learning rate, which itself contributes less than 1% to the total variance. The variance contributed by objects of interest is 81.9% of total variance, which is the same as in the substantial variance check of Table 3.8, modulo numerical errors of the estimator. According to the 80% threshold of Jiang [2018], this coefficient value tells us that predictions of the neural network are consistent across the meta-parameter configurations of the partial grid search. According to the guidelines of Koo and Li [2016], this value of φ can be interpreted as good reliability.

Returning to the question of the feasibility of variance component analysis for large meta-parameter configuration spaces, we propose the conjecture that a manual search over a partial meta-parameter grid exhibits higher variance due to meta-parameters than searching over a full grid. This rule of thumb suggests that human modelers actively search for the models with highest variation and are not interested in filling the gaps with models of similar performance to the already tested ones. This conjecture can be confirmed for our case by training an LMEM on data produced by evaluating a full grid of $3 \times 3 \times 2 \times 3 \times 3 = 162$ models instantiated to all combinations of basic meta-parameter values given in Table 3.7.

Let us apply a substantial variance on a random-effects-only model (3.15) trained on the dataset of fully crossed meta-parameter configurations. Proportions of substantial and residual variance in Table 3.10 are the same, modulo numerical approximation errors of the estimators, as in the full variance decomposition shown in Table 3.11 for the model (3.16). We see that in comparison to Table 3.9, variance components corresponding to sentences increased marginally

Table 3.9: Variance components in partial meta-parameter grid search for basic fine-tuning experiment of neural machine translation model on human marking data in Kreutzer et al. [2020]

Variance Component v	Variance σ_v^2	Percent
sentence s	0.0905	81.9
residual	0.0189	17.1
learning_rate	0.0008	0.72
decoder_dropout_hidden	0.000145	0.13
encoder_dropout	0.000108	0.1
random_seed	0.0000133	0.01
decoder_dropout	0.0000000000562	0

Table 3.10: Variance components for substantial variance check of full meta-parameter grid search for basic fine-tuning experiment of neural machine translation model on human marking data in Kreutzer et al. [2020]

Variance Component v	Variance σ_v^2	Percent
sentence s	0.109	86.0
residual	0.0177	14.0

Table 3.11: Variance components in full meta-parameter grid search for basic fine-tuning experiment of neural machine translation model on human marking data in Kreutzer et al. [2020]

Variance Component v	Variance σ_v^2	Percent
sentence s	0.109	85.9
residual	0.0173	13.7
learning_rate	0.000413	0.33
encoder_dropout	0.0000978	0.08
decoder_dropout	0.00000670	0.01
decoder_dropout_hidden	0.0000147	0.01
random_seed	0.00000166	0

Table 3.12: Variance components in extended meta-parameter grid search for basic fine-tuning experiment of neural machine translation model on human marking data in Kreutzer et al. [2020]

Variance Component v	Variance σ_v^2	Percent
sentence s	0.0902	76.8
residual	0.0246	20.9
learning_rate	0.00240	2.05
decoder_dropout	0.000120	0.1
encoder_dropout	0.0000543	0.05
decoder_dropout_hidden	0.0000314	0.03
random_seed	0.00000155	0

from 0.0905 to 0.109, while variance corresponding to meta-parameters and residual variance decreased. This results in a slightly higher reliability coefficient φ of 85.9%. Comparing this to the value $\varphi = 81.9\%$ for the partial grid search lets us interpret the latter as a conservative reliability estimate that is only improved if variance is smoothed out by filling in missing points in the grid.

Note that we purposely speak of a "rule of thumb" since no guarantee can be given for partial grid searches resulting in high meta-parameter variance. The same effect can also be obtained by extending the grid to include extreme values. For example, the basic grid in Table 3.7 can be extended with dropout values of 0, effectively turning off the regularization effect of dropout, and by adding too large learning rates, possibly introducing instability in training. A fully crossed configuration space containing all combinations of meta-parameter values results in $4 \times 4 \times 4 \times 4 \times 3 = 768$ trained models. We expect a variance component analysis on this extended grid to result in lower reliability coefficient values, due to the increased variance of more heterogeneous models being evaluated. The variance components of random-effects-only LMEM trained on the extended grid of meta-parameters is shown in Table 3.12. We see that the variance corresponding to learning rate and residual variance increase, while substantial variance is again a bit lower, resulting in a lower reliability coefficient φ of 76.8%.

Interactions between Meta-Parameters and Data. Another important use of LMEMs that goes beyond assessing meta-parameter "importance" by variance component analysis is investigating the interaction of meta-parameters and test data characteristics. Let us again consider the model that is fine-tuned on sentences annotated in "Marking" mode but now with the addition of weight assignment for marked and unmarked words as a meta-parameter. We consider two settings of this meta-parameter, called `delta_scheme`. The first option is symmetric negative

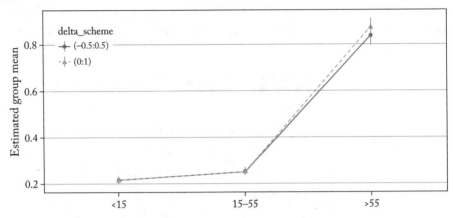

Figure 3.5: Estimated group mean of translation edit rate (TER) for neural machine translation models trained with meta-parameter weights $(-0.5, 0.5)$ vs. $(0, 1)$ for negative and positive markings.

and positive weights $(-0.5, 0.5)$ in the loss function for marked and unmarked words. The second option is a simpler scheme that ignores negatively marked words in training by applying weights $(0, 1)$ for marked and unmarked words, respectively. Our goal here is to assess the importance of the interaction between one particular meta-parameter setting and sentence length, in order to better understand evaluation results and to choose an appropriate setting for future applications.

In this experiment, the response variable Y to be modeled is the TER score measured for each sentence. Sentences are modeled as random effects v_s. Furthermore, we model the two settings of the weighting scheme for markings as fixed effect v_d. Source sentence length of the test data is divided into three bins of 1–14, 15–55, and > 55 words, and is modeled as fixed effect v_n. Our goal is to analyze interactions v_{nd} between the weighting scheme and sentence lengths as a fixed interaction effect. The following model

$$Y = v + v_s + v_n + v_d + v_{nd} + \epsilon_{residual} \qquad (3.17)$$

is estimated by encoding fixed and random effects in an LMEM. As can be seen from Figure 3.5, the choice of the weighting scheme causes a difference in TER evaluation score of the neural machine translation models for test sentences in the bracket of > 55 words.

Discussion. The basic components of model-based reliability testing discussed in this chapter date back to Fisher's [1925] statistical techniques for variance component analysis and intraclass correlation coefficients. We replace ANOVA methods by modern LMEMs for modeling and estimation [Wood, 2017], and use refined analysis techniques from psychometrics to design optimal measurement procedures [Brennan, 2001]. The psychometric literature includes a wide variety of further reliability measures which are too plentiful to be covered here. Standard correlation-based reliability coefficients like split-half reliability or the Spearman–Brown formula (see Lord and Novick [1968]) or Cronbach's coefficient alpha [Cronbach, 1951] can be reformulated as versions of ICCs (see Webb et al. [2006]), albeit under variance-restricting conditions that do not seem applicable to human annotators or to machine learning models. Well-known notions such as inter- or intra-rater reliability can easily be derived as special cases of ICCs (see Brennan [2001]). For example, in fully crossed designs including facets for raters r, instantiations i, and for interactions sr, si, and ri, with objects of measurement being sentences s, intra-rater reliability is calculated by fixing the rater facet to one rater, and generalizing over instantiations, without averaging:

$$\varphi_{intra-rater} = \frac{\sigma_s^2 + \sigma_{sr}^2}{\sigma_s^2 + \sigma_{sr}^2 + \sigma_{ri}^2 + \sigma_{residual}^2}. \tag{3.18}$$

In a similar way, inter-rater reliability is obtained by fixing the instantiations to one, and generalizing over raters, without averaging:

$$\varphi_{inter-rater} = \frac{\sigma_s^2 + \sigma_{si}^2}{\sigma_s^2 + \sigma_{si}^2 + \sigma_{sr}^2 + \sigma_{residual}^2}. \tag{3.19}$$

However, these measures are formulated in the spirit of relative reliability coefficients that do not provide an added value to the general coefficient φ and are harder to interpret. If the interest is to investigate additional factors like rater accuracy or sentence difficulty that further influence data annotation performance, Bayesian models of annotation are recommended [Passonneau and Carpenter, 2014, Paun et al., 2018].

Variance component analysis has been applied to information retrieval models [Ferro and Silvello, 2016, Robertson and Kanoulas, 2012, Voorhees et al., 2017] and machine learning models in general [Bergstra and Bengio, 2012, Hutter et al., 2014, Zimmer et al., 2020]. The former approaches focus on interactions between search queries modeled as random effects, and retrieval system components modeled as fixed effects, and they are based on variants of ANOVA for modeling. The latter approaches focus on meta-parameter importance, without considering interactions between meta-parameter settings and test data properties. They are based on functional ANOVA [Hutter et al., 2014] or Gaussian process regression [Bergstra and Bengio, 2012] of the function from meta-parameters to performance evaluation scores. None of the mentioned approaches take advantage of the flexibility of LMEMs to model meta-parameter variance by random effects.

A distinctive feature of our approach is the ICC-based idea of quantifying reliability by the proportion of variance attributable to the objects of interest. For our applications to NLP and data science, this requires evaluation metrics that are computed for each measurement object separately instead of summative evaluation scores as in the approaches of Hutter et al. [2014] or Bergstra and Bengio [2012]. Furthermore, it requires that the test data exhibit sufficient heterogeneity. This condition is naturally satisfied by the heterogeneity of patient data in medical data science where, for example, disease severity scores are measured for diseased and healthy patients. We believe that these requirements are also met in several NLP applications. For example, high performance on heterogeneous test data is a common requirement to assess the generalization ability of machine learning models in the area of machine translation [Barrault et al., 2020]. In this community, sentence-level evaluation metrics are preferred for the interpretability of the metrics, and to calculate sentence-level correlations with human judgments (see Rei et al. [2020] and Zhang et al. [2020] for recent examples).

3.4   NOTES ON PRACTICAL USAGE

The statistical methods presented in this chapter offer a variety of practical applications. Let us first consider reliability of data annotation performance. The reliability coefficient φ introduced in Definition 3.3 is recommended as replacement for the widely used α coefficient [Krippendorff, 2004] since it covers all advantages claimed for α (e.g., applicability to multiple raters, to all scales of measurement, and to data with missing values), without suffering any of its known disadvantages (see the paradoxa and abnormalities discussed in Section 3.3.1). Furthermore, it goes beyond the pure descriptive nature of α since it is formulated in a framework of statistical inference. The latter difference also bears a huge interpretational consequence: while a large α value is meant to indicate that the concrete annotations for a fixed set of objects obtained from a fixed set of raters agree higher than expected, a high value of φ makes a statement that transcends the sample at hand: it indicates that the variability in annotations is attributable to object differences, and not to irrelevant idiosyncrasies of raters or instantiations of annotations. Last, the reliability coefficient φ offers insights into the reasons for (lacking) reliability by explicit variance components, including raters, instantiations, and interactions between raters and data. This information can be used in exploratory studies that may suggest, for example, to average measurements across several raters, or to filter particular raters, for more reliable and still efficient annotation.

Considering model prediction performance, an important and well-established application of the techniques presented in this chapter is the use of variance component analysis in tandem with meta-parameter optimization [Hutter et al., 2014, Zimmer et al., 2020]. A variance component analysis of meta-parameters in a performance evaluation experiment for machine learning models allows an assessment of the importance of meta-parameters relative to each other, an assessment of variance due to interaction of meta-parameters and data, and an assessment of the change in variance of a meta-parameters across different budgets. For example, freezing meta-parameters with a smaller contribution to total variance, and paying special attention to meta-parameters causing larger variation, will aid more efficient meta-parameter optimization that makes best use of a given computational budget. Meta-parameter optimization itself is a separate topic that goes beyond the scope of this book (see, for example, Habelitz and Keuper [2020]).

A further recommendation is to establish the use of the reliability coefficient φ to assess the reliability of performance evaluation of machine learning models: reporting φ complementary to reporting the best achieved performance for a machine learning model on a test set allows relativizing reported high scores by the accrued variance due to extensive meta-parameter search. Overly large computational requirements to find best performing system settings will be revealed by a large variance component due to extensive meta-parameter searches, and systems yielding nominally lower performance score might be preferred because of their robustness against meta-parameter variation. A related problem is that of underspecifcation in machine learning [D'Amour et al., 2020], leading to instability and poor model behavior in certain test situations, depending on choices such as random seeds in training. Here a computation of reliability coefficients based on variance components allows assessing possible reasons for instability.

An advantage of the presented model-based techniques is the fact that they revolve around the decomposition of output variance on already existing performance evaluation scores of models obtained during meta-parameter optimization. The methods are applicable to arbitrary models and arbitrary tasks. For tasks with non-numeric outputs, the methods can be applied by introducing a numeric evaluation metric (e.g., edit distance in our machine translation examples) for every predicted label. The substantial variance check based on Proposition 3.6 allows a simple assessment of the amount of substantial variance for a given data, without having to conduct a full variance decomposition. Furthermore, estimation and statistical properties of LMEMs are well understood [Demidenko, 2013] and can build on well-established software packages like `lme4` [Bates et al., 2015]. Last, reliability analysis of meta-parameter variation is ideally complemented with likelihood ratio tests based on nested LMEM models [Pinheiro and Bates, 2000]—this will be the topic of the next chapter.

CHAPTER 4

Significance

Closely related to the problem of the reliability presented in the previous chapter is the problem of determining if the difference between multiple performance evaluation measurements is *statistically significant*. If the interest is in the statistical significance of differences between performance evaluation scores of machine learning models, the discussion of the previous chapter showed that there are two major sources of randomness that need to be respected: one is the randomness of the test data sample on which the models are to be compared. The other is the inherent randomness of the machine learning procedure, exemplified by meta-parameter variations.

Unfortunately, in state-of-the-art research following the train-dev-test paradigm, systematic uncertainty estimation is a neglected problem [Forde and Paganini, 2019], and statistical significance testing is often completely ignored. Instead, researchers frequently waive statistical significance tests in favor of rules of thumb for sufficiently large distances between observed evaluation scores. The thresholds are based on common wisdom in respective application areas. For example, in the area of machine translation, result differences of at least 1–2 BLEU points [Papineni et al., 2002] seem to be publication worthy and are often termed "significant" [Marie et al., 2021].

Since the advent of regular benchmark tests in machine translation, statistical significance tests have become more popular. However, there is a confusing multitude of tests without clear selection criteria, ranging from parametric tests like the t-test,[1] nonparametric versions of this tests like the sign test,[2] to sampling-based tests like the bootstrap test,[3] or the approximate randomization test.[4] Dror et al. [2020] present a table that matches the most common evaluation metrics in NLP to significance tests based on whether the evaluation metrics fulfill distributional assumptions required for parametric tests, or whether nonparametric or sampling-based tests have to be used.

The standard scenario is to compare the single best result, achieved by the model with the most extensive meta-parameter search, against a baseline system and evaluate both systems independently on a variety of test sets and language pairs. Besides the variety of significance tests to compare trained machine learning models on a single dataset, specialized techniques have

---

[1]This test is due to Student [1908]. NLP applications are discussed in Dror et al. [2020].

[2]See Larsen and Marx [2012] for the theory and Collins et al. [2005] for NLP applications.

[3]This test is due to Efron and Tibshirani [1993] and has been applied to NLP by Graham et al. [2014] and Koehn [2004].

[4]This test is also known under the name of permutation test, and dates back to Fisher [1935]. It has been applied to NLP by Clark et al. [2011], Riezler and Maxwell [2005], and Yeh [2000].

been presented for comparing models under multiple meta-parameter settings, based on their empirical score distributions [Dror et al., 2019], or by reporting bootstrap confidence intervals on performance evaluation scores [Henderson et al., 2018, Lucic et al., 2018]. Furthermore, techniques to incorporate variance due to datasets into the evaluation process have been suggested [Dror et al., 2017, Nadeau and Bengio, 1999]. However, none of these advanced techniques have yet found noticeable usage in NLP and data science evaluations. Thus, the problem of variance in performance evaluation measurements originating from different meta-parameter settings and varying properties of test data is largely ignored in significance testing in NLP and data science so far.

One of the goals of this chapter is to promote model-based significance testing using LMEMs, and to revitalize the generalized likelihood ratio test (GLRT) as a hypothesis test framework that shows its full potential in a model-based setting. GLRTs date back to the famous Neyman–Pearson theory of statistical testing [Neyman and Pearson, 1933], and provide a general hypothesis testing framework that applies to any evaluation metric, to multiple meta-parameter settings, and allows analyzing performance differences conditional on test data properties, something that can not be done with traditional tests. In the "nested models" setup [Pinheiro and Bates, 2000], first an LMEM is trained by maximum likelihood estimation on the performance scores of two machine learning models, each of which is trained itself under a variety of meta-parameter settings, and evaluated on a concatenation of different test sets. Then a GLRT assesses the statistical significance of a fixed "system" effect of the trained LMEM that differentiates between the models being compared. This provides a one-stop generalized approach to test the statistical significance of performance differences between two machine learning models, where variance in evaluation scores due to meta-parameters and test data characteristics is incorporated into the LMEM, without having to resort to specialized approaches in order to deal with multiple predictions and multiple datasets (see Dror et al. [2020], Chapters 4 and 5, respectively). Furthermore, the use of LMEMs for reliability analysis and significance testing reveals the intimate relationship between increased reliability of models and increased power of significance tests.

Another advantage of a model-based approach to significance testing is that it bypasses the discussion about matching types of significance tests to evaluation metrics in NLP (see Dror et al. [2020], Chapter 3). A model-based approach fits a wide range of evaluation metrics since the inference is now based on interpretable parameters of the LMEM (whose approximate distribution follows from maximum likelihood theory), and not on some quantity (whose distribution is unknown) that is directly calculated from the performance evaluation scores.

We begin this chapter with a short discussion of the principles of classical parametric significance testing and its shortcomings. Next, we address less obvious assumptions behind sampling-based significance tests that can severely limit the scope of their applicability. Finally, we discuss the workings of the GLRT and related tests, and showcase some of its advantages with our running example of interactive machine translation [Kreutzer et al., 2020].

4.1   PARAMETRIC SIGNIFICANCE TESTS

The fundamental goal of statistical significance testing is to decide between two mutually exclusive and exhaustive sets of hypotheses, one called the null hypothesis H_0 and the other called the alternative hypothesis H_1, by evidence obtained from observed random samples. Every statistical test, regardless if it is parametric, nonparametric, or sampling-based, starts by assuming the correctness of the null hypothesis and, based on this assumption, derives the distribution of a so-called test statistic[5] which is used to distinguish between H_0 and H_1. The crucial step is to derive the distribution of this statistic under the null hypothesis. If the observed value of the test statistic is very unlikely under H_0—lower or equal than a predefined significance level $\alpha \in (0, 1)$—the null hypothesis is rejected in favor of the alternative hypothesis.

For parametric tests it is sometimes possible to derive this distribution analytically,[6] based on the assumed data distribution and known parameters of this distribution. However, in most cases the distribution of the test statistic can only be approximated via asymptotic arguments. This is possible especially for test statistics which are based on sums of random variables.

Let us consider the problem of testing hypotheses about the expected value of a distribution F with finite expectation and non-zero variance. The key theorem that facilitates arriving at a useful distribution for a test about the mean is the Central Limit Theorem. The classical form can be stated in the following way.[7]

Theorem 4.1   (Classical Central Limit Theorem).   *Let $\bar{X}_N$ be the arithmetic mean of the first N of a sequence of independent and identically distributed scalar random variables $X_1, X_2, \ldots$. Let us further assume that $\mathbb{E}Y_i^2 < \infty$ (meaning that the data are drawn from a distribution with finite expectation μ and variance σ^2), and let F_N denote the cumulative distribution function (cdf) of $\sqrt{N}\,\frac{\bar{X}_N - \mu}{\sigma}$, then*

$$F_N(x) \xrightarrow{N \to \infty} \Phi(x), \qquad \forall x \in \mathbb{R},$$

where $\Phi(x)$ denotes the cdf of a standard Gaussian random variable. Note that the result also holds when σ is unknown, but can be replaced by a consistent estimator.

To conduct a hypothesis test about the test statistic of the mean, we use Theorem 4.1 to approximate the distribution of $\bar{X}_N$ by a Gaussian distribution. The correctness of this approximation increases as N increases. This statement about the approximate distribution of the mean of samples of size N can be given as follows:

$$\bar{X}_N \overset{app}{\sim} \mathcal{N}\left(\mu, \frac{\sigma^2}{N}\right). \tag{4.1}$$

---

[5]Following Larsen and Marx [2012], we define as test statistic any function of the observed data whose numerical value dictates whether H_0 is accepted or rejected.

[6]If this is possible, the corresponding test is usually called *exact*.

[7]Formal derivations and proofs for several variants of the asymptotic argument can be found in van der Vaart [1998], Chapter 2.

It is important to stress that the approximate normal distribution of the mean $\bar{X}_N$ as stated in (4.1) follows from Theorem 4.1, irrespective of the shape of the distribution from which the samples $X_1, X_2, \ldots$ are drawn.

Let us assume that we know the our data were drawn from a distribution with standard deviation σ, and that we want to test if the mean μ of this distribution equals μ_0 or not. Then, the null hypothesis reads

$$H_0 : \mu - \mu_0 = 0,$$

and the alternative hypothesis is

$$H_1 : \mu - \mu_0 \neq 0.$$

For concreteness, let us use an example from Cohen [1995] where we know $\sigma = 50$ and we want to test if the expected value of the data generating distribution is $\mu_0 = 25$. To test this hypothesis, we sample 100 observations from which we estimate a mean $\bar{x}$[8] of 15, yielding a Z-score[9] of

$$Z = \sqrt{N}\frac{\bar{x} - \mu_0}{\sigma} = \sqrt{100}\frac{15 - 25}{50} = -2.$$

Let us further assume that we want to control the Type I error[10] at $\alpha = .05$.[11] Figure 4.1 shows the shape of a standard normal distribution, which is the approximate distribution of our test static under the null hypothesis. Based on the nature of our hypothesis pair and our choice of α, we can partition the range of our test statistic in two regions. One is called the acceptance region which comprises all observable values of the test statistic that are deemed compatible with the null hypothesis. The second region is called the rejection region. This region is the set of all observable values of the test statistic which are deemed incompatible with the null hypothesis. When we observe a value in this set, we decide to reject the null hypothesis in favor of the alternative. The rejection region is constituted by the tails of the distribution, which for our test is $(-\infty, -1.96] \cup [1.96, \infty)$. In our case, the observed value $Z = -2$ is in the rejection region, so we know that obtaining this result by chance under H_0 is less than 5%. Thus, we decide to reject H_0 at an $\alpha = 0.05$ level and call the difference between $\bar{x}$ and μ_0 statistically significant.

A hypothesis test like the previous is called a two-sided test because the alternative hypothesis encompasses both possibilities $\mu < \mu_0$ and $\mu > \mu_0$. If it only encompasses one of these,

---

[8]In this case, $\bar{x}$ serves as a estimator for μ. This usage is justified by the law of large numbers. To stress this point some authors use the symbol $\hat{\mu}_N$ instead of $\bar{x}_N$.

[9]According to our definition of test statistic, following Larsen and Marx [2012], both $\bar{x}$ and Z qualify as test statistics.

[10]Type I error means that we decide to reject the null hypothesis based on our test, but actually the null hypothesis is the correct model.

[11]This means that given the null hypothesis is correct, we want to set the probability that our test makes a Type I error at 5%. If the null hypothesis contains more than one alternative, then α bounds the supremum of the probability that our test makes a Type I error of more than 5%. The ability to control the Type I error probability at a nominal rate is one of the most important properties of a statistical significance test.

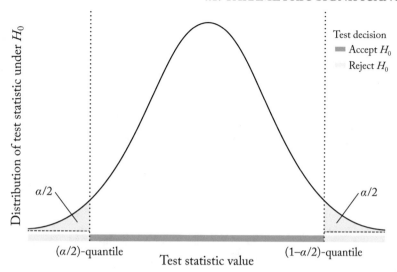

Figure 4.1: Critical region of two-tailed Z-test.

the corresponding test is called one-sided. Let us stay in the setting of the previous example, but now we are interested in testing whether μ is less than μ_0. The corresponding hypotheses pair reads:

$$H_0 : \mu \geq \mu_0$$
$$H_1 : \mu < \mu_0.$$

The test statistic is identical to the two-sided test, but the rejection region is different. As shown in Figure 4.2, we can put the total mass of α in the left tail, instead of splitting it as for a two-sided test. Thus, our rejection region now is $(-\infty, -1.64]$. Again, the observed value $Z = -2$ is in the rejection region, and we therefore decide to reject the null hypothesis and assume the alternative to be correct.

Discussion.   The workings behind the Z-test are similar to any parametric significance test. For a given test statistic, we need to know its sampling distribution. For the sum-based test statistic of the mean and for large enough sample sizes, we know that we can approximate the sampling distribution via a normal distribution by the Central Limit Theorem. Thus, for NLP and data science applications where the standard evaluation metric is based on a mean of sample evaluations, the family of approximate Z-tests allows us to test the statistical significance of result differences between performance evaluation of machine learning models.

One problem of applying the Central Limit Theorem to NLP and data science applications is the assumption of independence of the samples for which the test statistic of the mean

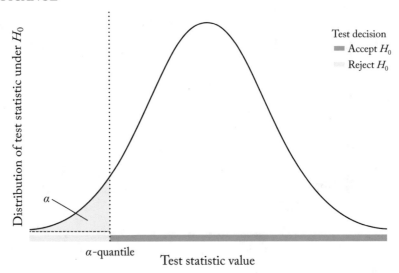

Figure 4.2: Critical region of left-tailed Z-test.

is calculated. This assumption is often violated in NLP and data science data if test sets consist of sentences of the same document.[12]

Another problem is the precise understanding of the phrase "mean of samples" that defines the test statistic in the Central Limit Theorem. This term applies to test statistics in NLP and data science that are calculated as means of evaluation scores that have been calculated separately for each sentence in a test set. Examples are accuracy scores for SOFA score prediction as used in Chapter 2, or the TER score [Snover et al., 2006] that we used to evaluate machine translation systems in Chapter 3. In general, any evaluation score that is computed as an average over sentence-level evaluation scores qualifies as a "mean" test statistic to which the Central Limit Theorem applies. Thus, no matter what the distribution of the sentence-wise evaluation score is, a significance test like the Z-test will be applicable to the test statistic of the mean of sentence-wise scores over the test set.

The story is different for corpus-wise evaluation measures such as BLEU [Papineni et al., 2002] that are computed on a corpus level, i.e., by accumulating all statistics for n-gram precision and brevity penalty over the whole test set and then combining these statistics in nonlinear way. In a similar way, corpus-level versions of precision, recall, or F1-score, where statistics on true positives, false positives, and false negatives are accumulated over the test items and then prorated, are nonlinear combinations of test statistics. Thus, even if the basic test statistic of n-gram

---

[12]The problem of clustered test samples is to be distinguished for another type of independence violations discussed in Yeh [2000]. These concern positive correlations between pairs of systems, e.g., a baseline and a refined system, for which significance of result differences is to be assessed. Yeh [2000] suggests tests for matched pairs as remedy. The model-based significance test discussed in the following can be seen as an instance of a matched-pair test.

counts, true positives, or false positives are normally distributed by virtue of being sums over statistics over test items, the nonlinear combination of normal distributions at the corpus level is no longer a proper mean test statistic in the sense of the Central Limit Theorem.

To summarize, since many standard performance evaluation measures in NLP and data science do not qualify as "mean of samples," techniques for statistical significance testing will be needed that can estimate sampling distributions for other test statistics, without reference to the Central Limit Theorem.[13] We will describe two such significance tests in the next section.

4.2   SAMPLING-BASED SIGNIFICANCE TESTS

4.2.1   BOOTSTRAP RESAMPLING

Bootstrap resampling has become a very popular technique for statistical significance testing in NLP and data science due to is ability to construct sampling distributions for virtually any test statistic, without knowing the its true sampling distribution and without making assumptions about the parametric distribution of the population. It has been developed in biostatistics [Efron and Tibshirani, 1993] and quickly been adopted in the machine learning community [Hastie et al., 2001]. In the following, we will restrict our attention to nonparametric bootstrap resampling, and refer to this technique with the shorthand "the bootstrap."

The intuition behind the bootstrap can be explained by the simplified principle that the sample itself is a representative "proxy" for the population, and that therefore a sampling distribution of the test statistic can be estimated by repeatedly sampling (with replacement) from the sample itself. In the following, we will consider bootstrap methods for the test statistic of the difference in corpus-level performance evaluation scores $S_A - S_B$ on a test set for machine learning models A and B. The null hypothesis is that the scores of systems A and B are random samples from the same distribution. First, the actual test statistic is computed on the test data. Next, the sample mean of the test statistic is computed on the bootstrapped data, i.e., the test statistic is computed on bootstrap samples of equal size to the test set, and averaged over bootstrap samples. In order to compute the sampling distribution of the test statistic under the null hypothesis, we employ the "shift" method described in Noreen [1989]. Here it is assumed that the sampling distribution of the null hypothesis and the bootstrap sampling distribution have the same shape but a different location. The location of the bootstrap sampling distribution is shifted so that it is centered at the location where the null hypothesis sampling distribution should be centered. This is achieved by subtracting the expected value of the score difference, estimated by the sample mean of the test statistic on the bootstrap samples, from each of its values. Then, a p-value is computed directly from the percentage of trials where the (shifted) test statistic is greater than or equal to the actual statistic. Thus, we directly compute the probability of obtaining a sample result under the null hypothesis that is as extreme or more extreme than

---

[13]The problem of corpus-level measures versus sentence-level measures often leads to confusion in attempts to match evaluation metrics to significance tests. For example, in the matching table of Chapter 3 of Dror et al. [2020], only sentence-level test statistics can be matched to parametric tests like the t-test, however, this assumption is not made explicit.

the score difference observed on the original test set. In accordance to standard practice in statistical significance testing, it is common to assess statistical significance at a given α level if the p-value is less than or equal to α. However, it is considered good practice to report p-values directly and treat them as the smallest α at which statistical significance can be assessed [McShane et al., 2019].

Pseudocode sketching a two-sided bootstrap test of significance of evaluation score differences is given below.

Algorithm 4.2 (Bootstrap Test)

Given test set outputs $(A_0, B_0) = (a_i, b_i)_{i=1}^N$, where a_i is the output of system $\mathcal{A}$, and b_i is the output of system $\mathcal{B}$, on test instance i.
Compute score difference $\Delta S_0 = S(A_0) - S(B_0)$ on test data.
For $k = 1, \ldots, K$:
    Generate bootstrap dataset $S_k = (A_k, B_k)$ by sampling N examples
    from $(a_i, b_i)_{i=1}^N$ with replacement.
    Compute score difference $\Delta S_k = S(A_k) - S(B_k)$ on bootstrap data.
Compute $\overline{\Delta S_k} = \frac{1}{K} \sum_{k=1}^K \Delta S_k$.
Set $c = 0$.
For $k = 1, \ldots, K$:
    If $|\Delta S_k - \overline{\Delta S_k}| \geq |\Delta S_0|$
       $c{+}{+}$
$p = c/K$.
Reject null hypothesis if p is less than or equal to specified rejection level α.

Discussion. The key assumption of the bootstrap can be described formally with Canty et al. [2006] as the *bootstrap substitution principle*. This principle states that an approximation of a probability distribution of the quantity $u(Y, F)$, where $Y = (Y_1, Y_2, \ldots, Y_N)$ is randomly sampled from F, can be constructed by replacing F by a resampling model $\hat{F}$ from which samples Y^* are drawn such that

$$P\{u(Y, F) \leq u|F\} \approx P\{u(Y^*, \hat{F}) \leq u|\hat{F}\}. \tag{4.2}$$

A standard nonparametric resampling model is the empirical distribution function $\tilde{F}$ which estimates the distribution F by assigning probability $1/N$ to each sample $Y_i, i = 1, \ldots, N$. The representativeness of the sample that is fundamental to the bootstrap can be measured by the size of the approximation error in the bootstrap substitution principle as the sample size N goes to infinity. This is called *bootstrap consistency* in Canty et al. [2006]. Bootstrap methods can be inconsistent if the left-hand side and the right-hand side of the bootstrap substitution Equation (4.2) do not converge to the same value, no matter how large the sample size is. Berg-Kirkpatrick et al. [2012] have shown that p-values computed on bootstrap samples from one test set may not be indicative of true result differences on another test set if there is a large domain shift between the test sets. This can be interpreted as an extreme case of inconsistency that is problematic for any statistical significance test, however, bootstrap inconsistency can result from complex interactions of resampling schemes, test statistics, and data distributions. Canty et al. [2006] describes various diagnostics for various types of bootstrap inconsistencies that are usually ignored in NLP and data science applications.

In contrast to our goal of incorporating randomness due to meta-parameters or test data into significance testing, bootstrap tests are usually applied to a single test set on which a pair of selected systems is to be compared. Sellam et al. [2021] presented a so-called "multi-bootstrap" technique that resamples both from random seeds and from instances of the test set, in order to estimate the significance of the result difference between average performance evaluation scores of two systems. In this setup, the more powerful and thus preferred paired design is only possible if random seeds are identical for compared systems, e.g., in fine-tuning setups. The unpaired design is more flexible, however, it suffers the usual loss in power since it has to assume zero covariance between the performance evaluation scores of the compared systems.[14]

4.2.2 PERMUTATION TESTS

The permutation test, also known as the (approximate) randomization test, dates back to Fisher [1935]. Similar to the bootstrap test, it is based on random sampling, however, it does not make an assumption of representativeness of the test sample that can be problematic in NLP data. Instead, it directly tests the weak assumption that two machine learning systems are related without, in fact, making an assumption about the population distribution of the evaluation scores either.

The null hypothesis of the permutation test is that systems A and B are identical. Thus, under the null hypothesis, outputs for the same input are exchangable, i.e., any output produced by one of the systems on a test sentence could have been produced just as likely by the other system. So shuffling the sentence-wise outputs between the two systems with equal probability, and recomputing the test statistic, allows approximating a p-value by computing the percentage of trials where the test statistic computed on the shuffled data is greater than or equal to the test statistic computed on the test data.

For a test set of N sentences there are 2^N different ways to shuffle the sentence-wise outputs between the two systems. If all permutations are considered, the randomization test is exact. Approximate randomization produces a subset of all possible shuffles, however, the more shuffles that are evaluated, the better the approximation of the p-value. Again, it is considered

---

[14]See, for example, the discussion of the two-sample t-test versus the paired sample t-test in Cohen [1995].

good practice to report p-values directly instead of just assessing statistical significance at a given α-level [McShane et al., 2019].

A sketch of an algorithm for a two-sided approximate randomization test for the significance of performance score differences is given below.

Algorithm 4.3   (Permutation Test)

Given test set outputs $(A_0, B_0) = (a_i, b_i)_{i=1}^{N}$, where the first element in the ordered pair (a_i, b_i) is the output of system $\mathcal{A}$, and the second element is the output of system $\mathcal{B}$, on test instance i.

Compute score difference $\Delta S_0 = S(A_0) - S(B_0)$ on test data.

Set $c = 0$.

For $r = 1, \ldots, R$:

Compute shuffled outputs (A_r, B_r) where for each $i = 1, \ldots, N$:

$$\mathrm{swap}(a_i, b_i) = \begin{cases} (a_i, b_i) & \text{with probability } 0.5, \\ (b_i, a_i) & \text{with probability } 0.5. \end{cases}$$

Compute score difference $\Delta S_r = S(A_r) - S(B_r)$ on shuffled data.

If $|\Delta S_r| \geq |\Delta S_0|$

$c + +$

$p = c/R$.

Reject null hypothesis if p is less than or equal to specified rejection level α.

Discussion.   The permutation test rests on the simple and powerful principle of *stratified shuffling* [Noreen, 1989] that allows generation of null-hypothesis conditions by shuffling outputs between the two systems at strata that partition the data. Based on this principle, the inventors of the bootstrap rate the permutation test as follows:

> When there *is* something to permute, [...] it is a good idea to do so, even if other methods like the bootstrap are also brought to bear. [Efron and Tibshirani, 1993]

This statement showcases both the advantages and disadvantages of the permutation test. In order to generate null-hypothesis conditions, strata for shuffling outputs between the two systems have to be identified. Strata are given naturally in NLP test sets where each sentence corresponds to a stratum at which the system outputs can be permuted. These outputs can be sentence-wise evaluation scores or count statistics that are accumulated over the whole test corpus, for example, sentence-level TER [Snover et al., 2006] or sentence-level n-gram counts in BLEU [Papineni et al., 2002], respectively. If the goal is to compare two machine learning systems on the same sentences of a test set, a permutation test is easily implemented and it allows to assess statistical significance with great power (i.e., high probability of rejecting H_0 when it is false). The latter has been shown formally in a comparison of permutation tests to parametric tests for large samples [Hoeffding, 1952].

However, the stratified shuffling principle can also be a restriction since sampling without replacement does not simulate drawing samples from an infinite population. The permutation test thus does not allow approximating a sampling distribution of the test statistic, as is done in the bootstrap test. The upside of not making the assumption of representativeness of the sample is that the permutation test makes fewer Type I errors (i.e., rejecting H_0 when it is true) and fewer Type II errors (i.e., not rejecting H_0 when it is false) than the bootstrap if consistency of the latter is not given. This has been shown experimentally in Noreen [1989] and Riezler and Maxwell [2005].

To sum up, the permutation test seems to be the method of choice if the only goal is to assess the statistical significance of a difference in evaluation scores between two systems on the same test set. However, in order to apply a permutation test as described above, a single configuration of meta-parameters has to be chosen for each system, and a single dataset needs to be fixed. This scenario is too restrictive in light of the work that we presented in Chapter 3, since it ignores known sources of variance in performance evaluation of machine learning models. A notable exception is the approach of Clark et al. [2011] that includes multiple optimizer replications into a permutation test by permuting like hypothesis between systems and optimization runs. This procedure retains the power of the permutation test as long as small numbers of pairwise comparisons are conducted, but it increases the probability of Type I errors for larger numbers of pairwise comparisons.[15] A more flexible framework for statistical significance testing that allows multiple comparisons without increased Type I error, and enables an elegant incorporation of variability due to optimization and test data, is the model-based approach to significance testing. We will describe this technique in the next section.

4.3   MODEL-BASED SIGNIFICANCE TESTING

The central property of model-based significance testing is the fact that the hypotheses to be tested concern parameters of probability distributions. This allows us to fit probability models such as LMEMs to performance evaluation data of two machine learning models, and to compare the two underlying systems via the corresponding parameter in the LMEMs trained on the respective evaluation results. The test of choice in this paradigm is the (generalized) likelihood ratio test that dates back to Neyman and Pearson [1933]. We will follow the exposition in van der Vaart [1998].

---

[15]See, for example, the discussion of multiple comparisons in Larsen and Marx [2012].

4.3.1   THE GENERALIZED LIKELIHOOD RATIO TEST

The hypotheses to be tested in a likelihood ratio test are hypotheses about parameters of probability distributions. Suppose we observe a sample $Y = (Y_1, Y_2, \ldots, Y_N)$ from a probability distribution p_θ, and we wish to test the null hypothesis

$$H_0 : \theta \in \Theta_0,$$

against the alternative hypothesis

$$H_1 : \theta \in \Theta_1.$$

If both hypotheses consist of single points θ_0 and θ_1, then a most powerful test can be based on the test statistic of the likelihood ratio

$$\frac{\prod_{i=1}^{N} p_{\theta_0}(Y_i)}{\prod_{i=1}^{N} p_{\theta_1}(Y_i)},$$

by the Neyman–Pearson lemma [Neyman and Pearson, 1933].

An extension of the Neyman–Pearson theory replaces single points by the supremum over a restricted parameter space Θ_0 for the null hypothesis, and by the supremum over the whole parameter space $\Theta = \Theta_0 \cup \Theta_1$ for the alternative hypothesis, leading to the generalized likelihood ratio statistic

$$\frac{\sup_{\theta \in \Theta_0} \prod_{i=1}^{N} p_\theta(Y_i)}{\sup_{\theta \in \Theta} \prod_{i=1}^{N} p_\theta(Y_i)} = \frac{l_0}{l_1},$$

that builds the basis of the generalized likelihood ratio test. Larsen and Marx [2012] describe the test in the following succinct form.

Algorithm 4.4   (Generalized Likelihood Ratio Test (GLRT))   Reject H_0 if the generalized likelihood ratio statistic

$$\lambda = \frac{l_0}{l_1},$$

has a value

$$0 < \lambda \leq \lambda^*$$

where λ^* is chosen such that $P(0 < \lambda \leq \lambda^* | H_0 \text{ is true }) = \alpha$ for a significance level α.

The null hypothesis of the GLRT is the assumption that the restricted model l_0 explains the data adequately. Since $0 < \lambda \leq 1$, the intuition behind the test is that values of λ close to 1 suggest that the restricted model assumed under H_0 explains the data as well as a more complex model assumed under H_1, thus H_0 should be accepted for such values of λ. Conversely, values of λ close to 0 suggest that the data are not very compatible with the parameter values in the restricted model, thus H_0 should be rejected in favor of H_1, which more adequately explains the data.

In order to determine the critical value λ^* for a given significance level α, we need to know the distribution of the test statistic λ. Fortunately, our test statistic is based on maximum likelihood estimates of parameters of a probability distribution—in our case, we will employ the parametric family of LMEMs that we already used for reliability assessment in Chapter 3— and we can fall back on an asymptotic result similar to the Central Limit Theorem, this time a theorem showing the asymptotic normality of maximum likelihood estimates.[16]

Theorem 4.5 (Asymptotic Distribution of Maximum Likelihood Estimators). *Let $Y = (Y_1, Y_2, \ldots, Y_N)$ be sample from a probability distribution p_θ, and define the log-likelihood of the sample as $\ell_N(\theta) = \log \prod_{i=1}^{N} p_\theta(Y_i)$. If the maximum likelihood estimator $\hat{\theta}$ exists as the solution to the equation $\frac{\partial}{\partial \theta} \ell_N(\theta) = 0$, in addition to second and third derivatives of $\ell_N(\theta)$, then the asymptotic distribution of $[N \cdot I_N(\theta)]^{1/2}(\hat{\theta} - \theta)$ is the standard normal distribution, where $I_N(\theta) = \mathbb{E}_{p_\theta}[(\frac{\partial}{\partial \theta} l_N(\theta))^2]$ is the Fisher information of the sample Y about θ.*

Similar to the Central Limit Theorem 4.1, we consequently get a statement on the approximate distribution of $\hat{\theta}$ being the multivariate normal distribution with mean θ and variance $[N \cdot I_N(\theta)]^{-1}$:

$$\hat{\theta} \stackrel{app}{\sim} \mathcal{N}(\theta, [N \cdot I_N(\theta)]^{-1}). \tag{4.3}$$

Using Theorem 4.5, it can be shown that under the null hypothesis the distribution of the statistic $-2 \log \lambda$ is asymptotically chi squared-distributed. This result is due to Wilks [1938]. We present a derivation of the asymptotic distribution of the likelihood ratio statistic for the simple case of a single random variable Y and a scalar-valued parameter θ in Appendix A.3.[17] In short, the result states that the random variable W, defined as

$$W = -2 \log \Lambda = 2 \log \frac{l_1(Y_1, \ldots, Y_N)}{l_0(Y_1, \ldots, Y_N)} \stackrel{app}{\sim} \chi^2_{df = k_1 - k_0}, \tag{4.4}$$

follows a χ^2 distribution with $k_1 - k_0$ degrees of freedom if the general model yielding l_1 has k_1 parameters and the restricted model yielding l_0 has k_0 parameters. This allows us to reject H_0 if the observed value w of W is greater than the $(1 - \alpha)$-quantile of the aforementioned

---

[16]Derivations and proofs for variants of the asymptotic argument can be found in van der Vaart [1998], Chapter 7.

[17]A detailed proof is given in van der Vaart [1998], Chapter 16.

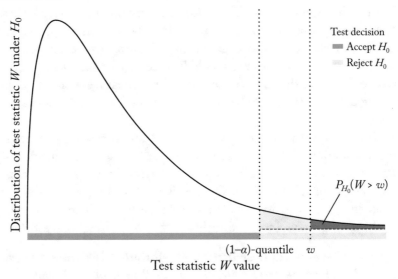

Figure 4.3: p-value based on χ^2 distribution.

distribution, that is, if the p-value

$$p := P_{H_0}(W > w) \tag{4.5}$$

is smaller than the rejection level α. The critical region of the χ^2 distribution is illustrated in Figure 4.3. Again, since the p-values can be calculated directly, it is good practice to report the p-value instead of assessing the statistical significance at a given α-level [McShane et al., 2019].

4.3.2 LIKELIHOOD RATIO TESTS USING LMEMS

The Nested Models Setup

Let us reconsider the experiments on interactive machine translation by Kreutzer et al. [2020] that we used to illustrate reliability of model prediction performance in Chapter 3. The machine learning objective of this study was to fine-tune neural machine translation systems on either machine-translated sentences annotated with human markings or human post-edits of machine translations. For the purpose of reliability assessment, we trained a random-effects-only LMEM on response variables Y consisting of TER scores for a multitude of RNN models fine-tuned under different meta-parameter settings evaluated on 1,041 test sentences.[18] The purpose of significance testing is to assess the statistical significance of observed differences in TER scores between the baseline model and the models fine-tuned on markings or post-edits, respectively.

Let us first have a look at the TER evaluation score in a boxplot shown in Figure 4.4. The

---

[18]Note that 2 of the 1,043 test sentences reported in Kreutzer et al. [2020] were duplicates that we removed in our LMEM experiments.

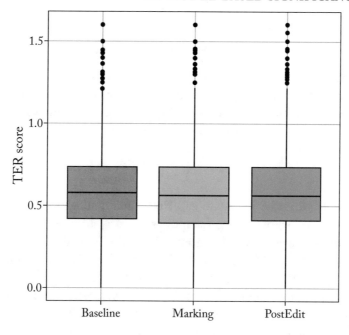

Figure 4.4: Median TER scores for baseline and machine translation systems fine-tuned on markings or post-edits.

horizontal line in the middle of the box marks the median value of the data points in the specific group. The box indicates the range where the middle 50% of the data points are located. The vertical lines are called whiskers and serve the purpose to identify observations with unusually large or small values in the data set (so-called outliers) which are represented by point-like symbols below or above the whisker. Figure 4.4 shows that the shape of the box plot is rather similar for all three systems, with the boxplots for "Marking" and "PostEdit" being located slightly below the "Baseline" boxplot. This means that by central tendency, both feedback methods yield slightly improved translation quality.

Let us conduct a first-cut analysis of the statistical significance of the observed evaluation results. We assume that, for the moment, we are only interested in the statistical significance of the observed result difference between the baseline system and the model fine-tuned on markings. Since each of the latter RNN models was trained three times with different random seeds, in a first, conventional approach we simply average the TER scores for the models trained on human annotations, and assess the statistical significance of the average result differences to the baseline results. The simplest modeling approach is to specify an LMEM that realizes a standard linear model as in (4.6) and train it on data collected from evaluation scores for both systems. For the response variable Y consisting of TER scores for each test sentence, we get the following model:

$$Y = \mu + v_m \cdot \mathbb{I}_m + \epsilon_{residual}. \qquad (4.6)$$

The model specifies a fixed effect μ for the baseline grand mean and uses an indicator function $\mathbb{I}_m$ to activate a fixed effect v_m that represents the deviation of the fine-tuning on markings from the baseline. In order to conduct a GLRT, we set up the restricted model in (4.7), a special case of model (4.6) where the factor v_m is restricted to be zero, and train it on the same data as model (4.6):

$$Y = \mu + \epsilon_{residual}. \qquad (4.7)$$

This setup of *nested models* [Pinheiro and Bates, 2000] allows us to conduct a GLRT with the restricted model (4.7) representing the null hypothesis, the more general model (4.6) representing the alternative hypothesis, and model (4.7) being nested within model (4.6). In our case, the null hypothesis model (4.7) assumes that there is no difference in the TER scores between the systems, and thus it estimates the mean TER score over the performance evaluation data of baseline and fine-tuned models. The alternative hypothesis model (4.6) specifies a fixed effect that represents the deviation of the TER scores of the fine-tuned model from the baseline, and the GLRT assesses the statistical significance of this fixed effect.

An analogous setup could be done for a system fine-tuned on post-edits by setting up a linear model (4.8) that specifies a fixed effect v_p for the deviation of fine-tuning on post-edits to the baseline.

$$Y = \mu + v_p \cdot \mathbb{I}_p + \epsilon_{residual}. \qquad (4.8)$$

As null hypothesis model we can use a model of the form (4.7) and train it on data of evaluation scores for baseline and post-edit tuned systems. This model then estimates the mean TER score over these data. Then we conduct a GLRT with the null hypothesis model (4.7) being nested within the alternative hypothesis model (4.8).

If our interest is only to test the hypothesis whether all three systems perform equally, we could set up a model (4.9) that incorporates both fixed effects v_m and v_p that are activated by indicator functions $\mathbb{I}_m$ and $\mathbb{I}_p$, respectively, representing the deviation of the fine-tuning on markings to the baseline, and the deviation of the fine-tuning on post-edits to the baseline. This model is trained on evaluation results of all three systems.

$$Y = \mu + v_m \cdot \mathbb{I}_m + v_p \cdot \mathbb{I}_p + \epsilon_{residual}. \qquad (4.9)$$

In order to test whether all three systems perform equally, we need to retrain the null hypothesis model (4.7) on the same data from all three systems. This model then estimates the mean TER score over the evaluation scores produced by all three models.

On the data from Kreutzer et al. [2020], a GLRT which compares model (4.9) against the restricted model (4.7) yields a p-value of 0.517. According to a standard significance level of 0.05, this result is too high to reject the null hypothesis that the three systems have equal performance. Do we have to conclude that the difference in performance evaluations between the three systems is not statistically significant? Or are our linear models too simple to adequately analyze our performance evaluation data? We will see that two important modifications to our setup that utilize the full power of LMEMs will yield a completely different picture than our first-cut analysis.

Multiple Comparisons and Meta-Parameter Variation

First, we realize that the simple linear models do not correctly represent the design of the experiment. Kreutzer et al. [2020] evaluated the three systems on the same sentence, once for the baseline system, and three times for each of the fine-tuned systems (one replication for each of three random seeds). Thus, each sentence was translated seven times in total. The simple linear models are instead based on a design that assumes that each system was evaluated once on a disjoint set of sentences. This forced us to average over replications, thereby losing useful information contained in the repeated measurements.

LMEMs allow us to better reflect the experiment design and to leverage this information by adding a random effect v_s for each sentence. The repeated measurements allow us to group the systems at the sentence level. Technically such a model treats sentences as random samples from a larger population and it incorporates an individual baseline deviation for each sentence. Thus, the model can decompose the total variance in three blocks: systematic variance due to the fixed effects of the model, variance due to sentence heterogeneity, and unexplained residual variance. This allows us to reduce the as of yet unaccounted residual variance by attributing a variance component σ_s^2 to variance between sentences. If we think of the residual error as noise that masks the signal of measured performance scores, we can effectively perform a noise reduction that increases the power of our tests to detect significant differences. We can also see that decreasing residual variance and increasing substantial variance corresponds to increasing the reliability coefficient φ of a model, thus relating increased reliability to increased power.

A second problem results from the multiple pairwise comparisons that would have to be done if we wanted to assess statistical significance of pairwise result differences, i.e., baseline vs. marking, baseline vs. post-edit, and marking vs. post-edit. This well-known problem of multiple comparisons yields an increase of the probability of Type I errors, i.e., the probability of randomly assessing statistical significance for result differences in k-fold pairwise comparisons grows exponentially in k. Recall that for a pairwise comparison of systems at $\alpha = 0.05$ means that the probability of incorrectly rejecting the null hypothesis that the systems are not different be less than 0.05. For a probability α_c of incorrectly rejecting the null hypothesis in a specific pairwise comparison, the probability α_e of at least once incorrectly rejecting the null hypothesis in an experiment involving k pairwise comparisons is

$$\alpha_e = 1 - (1 - \alpha_c)^k.$$

Table 4.1: Effect of model design on variance and significance

Design	General Model	Restricted Model	Residual	p-Value
average replications per random seed	Eq. (4.9)	Eq. (4.7)	0.2576	0.517
group replications at sentence level	Eq. (4.10)	Eq. (4.11)	0.05905	< 0.0001

For large values of k, the probability of concluding result differences incorrectly at least once is undesirably high. For example, in benchmark testing of 15 systems, $15(15-1)/2 = 105$ pairwise comparisons will have to be conducted. At a per-comparison rejection level $\alpha_c = .05$ this results in an per-experiment error $\alpha_e = .9954$, i.e., the probability of at least one spurious assessment of significance is $1 - (1 - .05)^{105} = .9954$. One possibility to reduce the likelihood that one or more differences assessed in pairwise comparisons is spurious is to run the comparisons at a more stringent per-comparison rejection level. A standard remedy for this problem is the *Bonferroni correction* (see DeGroot and Schervish [2012], Chapter 11) that corrects the per-comparison significance level $\frac{\alpha_c}{N_C}$ by the number of pairwise comparisons N_C. This will work fine for a small number of pairwise comparisons. For example, it would require a reasonable per-comparison rejection level $\alpha_c = 0.0167$ to reach a per-experiment error rate less than $\alpha_e = 0.05$ for 3 pairwise comparisons, but it would require reducing α_c to the point where a result difference has to be unrealistically large to be significant for larger numbers of pairwise comparisons.

Another solution to control the per-experiment error rate is the *Tukey test* that assumes that all mean factors are from same normal population as null hypothesis $H_0 : \mu_1 = \mu_2 = \cdots = \mu_k$, and conducts a significance test against the alternative hypothesis $H_1 : \mu_i \neq \mu_j$, for all $i \neq j$ in a single procedure (see Larsen and Marx [2012], Chapter 12).

Let us now incorporate the two discussed modifications—adding random effects for repeated measurements on sentences and conducting pairwise comparisons in a single procedure—into our model of the performance evaluation experiment for interactive machine translation. This will lead to an LMEM (4.10) that includes a random effect v_s for sentences and fixed effects v_m and v_p. Remember that v_m and v_p are activated by indicator functions $\mathbb{I}_m$ and $\mathbb{I}_p$, respectively, and represent the deviation from the baseline for fine-tuning on markings or post-edits:

$$Y = \mu + v_s + v_m \cdot \mathbb{I}_m + v_p \cdot \mathbb{I}_p + \epsilon_{residual}. \tag{4.10}$$

The restricted model (4.11) representing the null hypothesis in the GLRT only specifies a global mean μ and a sentence-specific deviation v_s, while restricting the other factors to zero:

$$Y = \mu + v_s + \epsilon_{residual}. \tag{4.11}$$

As repeated in Table 4.1, we found that a comparison of models (4.9) to (4.7) where we averaged replications of measurements per random seed without utilizing a random sentence

Table 4.2: p-values for pairwise TER differences between systems on test set

	p-Value
baseline – marking	< 0.0001
baseline – post-edit	< 0.0001
marking – post-edit	0.1625

variance effect v_s, yielded a p-value of 0.517. This was too high to reject the null hypothesis that the three systems have equal performance. Adding the random effect v_s reduces the residual error from 0.2576–0.05905, and yields a p-value < 0.0001 for a comparison of models (4.10) to (4.11). Thus, we can assess statistical significance of the difference between the three systems if sentence variance is taken into account.

Furthermore, the pairwise comparison shown in Table 4.2 yields significant differences between baseline and fine-tuning on markings ($p < 0.0001$), between baseline and fine-tuning on post-edits ($p < 0.0001$), but not for the comparison between fine-tuning on markings and fine-tuning on post-edits ($p = 0.1625$).

Dependency of Significance on Data Properties
In a further step, we would like to investigate if perhaps difference between baseline and fine-tuning modes, or even between fine-tuning modes, is dependent on certain properties of the test data. Similar to the analysis of the interaction of the meta-parameter `delta_scheme` with sentence length presented in Chapter 3, we will investigate whether the choice between baseline or fine-tuning modes depends on the length (measured in words) of the source language sentence. To get a first impression, we create a scatter plot with source sentence length on the x-axis and TER of the translation on the y-axis for all systems. Figure 4.5 shows that for all three systems, the contour lines of the point cloud are rather similar, and the relation between TER and source sentence length is increasing. We see an increase in TER for short sentences (< 15 words), followed by a rather flat section for sentences of length 15–55 words, and a steep increase for very long sentences (> 55 words). To emphasize this point, we classify the sentence length in three categories "short" (< 15), "typical" (15–55), and "very long" (> 55) and create boxplots of the data. Figure 4.6 highlights the observation that most of the improvement gained from human feedback happens for very long sentences, and to a lesser degree for very short ones, with no noticeable improvement for sentences of moderate length. Furthermore, we see that while the three systems behave nearly identical for typical sentences, they show noticeable differences for short and very long sentences.

In order to test this hypothesis, we extend model (4.10) by including a fixed effect v_n for sentence length, and fixed effects v_{nm} and v_{np} to analyze interactions between system choice

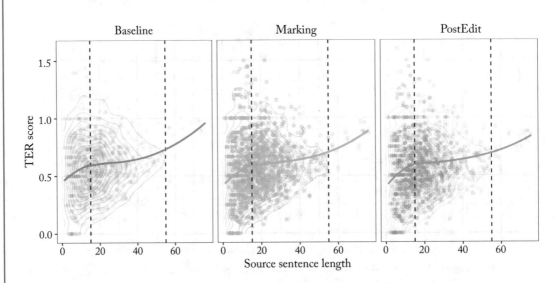

Figure 4.5: TER scores for baseline and machine translation systems fine-tuned on markings or post-edits, plotted against source sentence length.

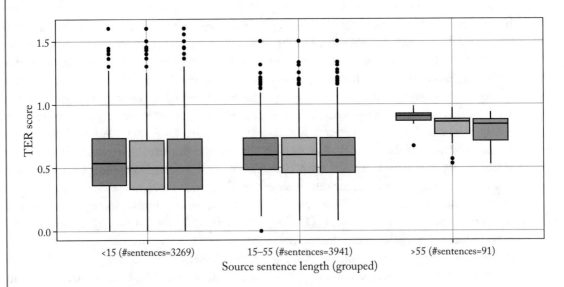

Figure 4.6: TER scores for baseline and machine translation systems fine-tuned on markings or post-edits, plotted against three bins of source sentence length.

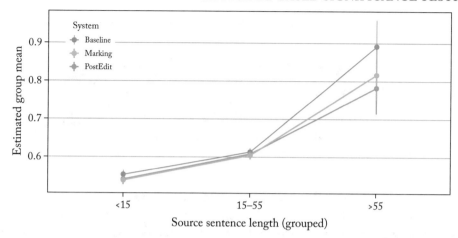

Figure 4.7: Interaction plot of estimated TER scores for baseline and machine translation systems fine-tuned on markings or post-edits and bins of source sentence length.

and sentence lengths, yielding model (4.12):

$$Y = \mu + \nu_s + \nu_n + (\nu_m + \nu_{nm}) \cdot \mathbb{I}_m + (\nu_p + \nu_{np}) \cdot \mathbb{I}_p + \epsilon_{residual}. \qquad (4.12)$$

A GLRT that compares model (4.12) to a null hypothesis model of the form

$$Y = \mu + \nu_s + \nu_n + \epsilon_{residual}. \qquad (4.13)$$

shows that there is a statistically significant difference ($p < 0.0001$) in evaluation scores between the three systems depending on the sentence length bins. This result is highlighted in the interaction plot given in Figure 4.7 that directly displays the estimated group means of TER score for each of the bins of source sentence length.

Figure 4.7 clearly shows that the biggest improvements are gained for long sentences, and fine-tuning on post-edits seems to outperform fine-tuning on markings for the experiment of Kreutzer et al. [2020]. In order to test this set of hypotheses, we perform pairwise comparisons between systems nested within source sentence length levels. These results are shown in Table 4.3.

In comparison to the result in Table 4.2 that we obtained without grouping sentences into length bins, Table 4.3 shows statistically significant differences between TER scores of marking and post-edit systems on very long sentences. Furthermore, for short sentences both systems show a significant improvement over the baseline model, but for typical sentences only the improvement of the marking system over the baseline is statistically significant. These results suggest that there is no uniform superiority of one feedback mode over the other and that an investigation into the interaction of feedback modes with data properties reveals important patterns.

Table 4.3: *p*-values for pairwise differences between systems on source sentences of different length

	Short	Typical	Very Long
baseline – marking	< 0.0001	0.0175	0.0003
baseline – post-edit	0.0002	0.2098	< 0.0001
marking – post-edit	0.2683	0.3052	0.0252

Discussion.   A unique theoretical feature of the proposed model-based approach to significance testing is that it mutes the old question of which significance test is appropriate for which evaluation measure. In a model-based paradigm, one does not have to bother with the distributional properties of complex evaluation measures since they are not treated directly as test statistics of a significance test. Instead, they are simply the response variables in the performance evaluation data on which LMEMs are trained. We can reuse already existing performance evaluation data, obtained by repeated measurements of evaluation scores of model variants, and perform a significance test on the parameter of an LMEM that incorporates the variability in the models and data.

Independent of the evaluation measure used, the test statistic of the GLRT is based on the parameter estimates of the LMEM trained on the performance evaluation data. It is a well-established result from maximum likelihood theory that the parameter estimates obtained by maximizing the likelihood asymptotically follow a normal distribution. Based on this fact it can be shown that the generalized likelihood ratio test statistic asymptotically follows a χ^2 distribution, which in turn allows to compute *p*-values for wide range of hypotheses including the typical A-B testing hypotheses pair. It should be mentioned that, while our model-based approach used GLRTs, other significance test on fixed effects of LMEMs are possible. For example, Pinheiro and Bates [2000] recommend *F*-tests or *t*-tests to avoid anti-conservative behavior of GLRTs, while Robertson and Kanoulas [2012] or Barr et al. [2013] do not find a Type I error inflation for GLRTs. In a similar way, model-based significance testing does not depend on the use of LMEMs, but other mixed effects models such as generalized additive mixed models [Wood, 2011] would also fit our purpose.

The key practical feature of the proposed model-based approach is that it unifies special-purpose significance tests for particular evaluation metrics, meta-parameter variations, and multiple test data into a single framework for hypothesis testing. Special-purpose approaches have been presented by Dror et al. [2019] to compare models under different meta-parameter settings by comparing their empirical score distribution, or by Dror et al. [2017] to perform multiple-hypothesis testing for multiple datasets. The idea of treating test data as random effects and thus increasing the power of statistical significance testing has already proposed by Robertson and Kanoulas [2012] for the area of information retrieval. However, the general applicability of LMEMs and GLRTs for significance testing under variations of meta-parameters and data properties has not yet been fully recognized in the wider community of NLP and data science research.

Last, our proposed frame work exhibits an intimate relationship between significance testing and reliability analysis where increased reliability of models implies higher power in detecting significant differences between them. Out of the main factors that influence the power of a test [Card et al., 2020, Larsen and Marx, 2012]—the significance level α, the variance of an effect, and the test set size—only the test set size is usually tuned by the experiment (dataset) designer. A reliability analysis provides a tool that allows identifying possible reasons for low power by an analysis of variance of model components.

4.4   NOTES ON PRACTICAL USAGE

The statistical significance tests presented in this chapter—and more variants of parametric, nonparametric, and sampling-based test procedures—have been discussed elsewhere, for example, in Dror et al. [2020]. Our main contribution is to put some of the earliest significance tests—the permutation test [Fisher, 1935] and the likelihood ratio test [Neyman and Pearson, 1933, Wilks, 1938]—into the limelight and showcase their general applicability to any task and evaluation metric in NLP and data science.

The permutation test achieves this goal without loss of power compared to parametric tests in standard settings [Hoeffding, 1952], and with the only limitation that it requires the selection of a pair of models under fixed meta-parameter settings for which the significance of a result difference is to be assessed. A notable exception is the permutation test of Clark et al. [2011] that allows incorporating multiple optimizer runs, however, this framework is restricted to small numbers of pairwise comparisons, it lacks the ability to differentiate significance testing according to properties of the test data.

A unified framework for statistical significance testing under variations on meta-parameter or data properties is offered by the model-based framework of GLRTs. The main idea of model-based significance testing is using statistical models like LMEMS, trained on test data performance evaluation scores of machine learning systems, and apply the nested models setup of GLRTs for significance testing. This setup allows the incorporation of variability into significance testing by clustering repeated measurements obtained from different meta-parameter configurations on the sentence level. Thus, it allows accounting for uncertainty introduced by the random nature of the training process. We showcased this advantage on the example of multiple training runs starting from different random seeds. The clustering of repeated measurements on the sentence level is suitable when (A) system are trained with the same meta-parameter values, (B) systems are trained with different meta-parameter values, and (C) if the meta-parameters of the systems differ.

The distinctive advantage of the model-based framework compared to extensions of bootstrap [Sellam et al., 2021] or permutation [Clark et al., 2011] tests to incorporate meta-parameter variation is that it enables analyzing significance of result differences conditional on data properties. We showcased this advantage by using a test set in our interactive machine translation example [Kreutzer et al., 2020] that consists of 30 selected TED talks on a variety of topics, and by analyzing significance separately for data properties like source sentence length. The latter analysis has the same goal as using heuristic test data splits, for example, based on sentence length [Søgaard et al., 2021], for improved performance evaluation of machine learning models. However, our approach allows the incorporation of factors of interest in the design of an LMEM trained on the whole performance evaluation dataset, instead of requiring separate runs of training and evaluation on the individual data splits.

The clustering of repeated measurements on the sentence level is a default option that can be extended if systems share other facets of variation, for example, if they are minor variations of each other and share other meta-parameter facets. Furthermore, similar to analyzing the dependency of significance on test sentence properties, indicators for test sets themselves can be used to analyze the dependency of significance on domains or topics of test sets.

APPENDIX A

Mathematical Background

A.1 GENERALIZED ADDITIVE MODELS

A.1.1 GENERAL FORM OF MODEL

Generalized additive models (GAMs) are an additive combination of smooth functions $f_k(x_k)$ of input *features* x_k (usually called predictor *covariates* by statisticians). These smooth functions are called *feature shapes* in the machine learning literature (or *smoothers* in the statistical community). They decompose a multivariate function into one-dimensional components f_k that can be nonlinear themselves. GAMs are called interpretable[1] models since the contribution of each feature x_k to the prediction can be interpreted by visualizing feature shapes via plotting $f_k(x_k)$ against x_k.

Given a data point $(\mathbf{x}^n, y^n)$ from data set $\{(\mathbf{x}^n, y^n)\}_{n=1}^N$, where $\mathbf{x} = (x_1, \ldots, x_p)$ is a p-dimensional real-valued vector of covariates, x_k denotes a component of $\mathbf{x}$, Y is a real valued random response variable from the exponential family, and $g(\cdot)$ is a nonlinear link function, the general form of a GAM can be given as follows:

$$g(\mathbb{E}[Y|\mathbf{x}]) = \sum_{k=1}^p f_k(x_k) + \sum_{i \neq j} f_{ij}(x_i, x_j).$$

There are many ways to realize a GAM. For example, Hastie and Tibshirani [1990] utilize nonparametric regression models, Lou et al. [2012] use boosted regression trees, Agarwal et al. [2020] introduce restrictions to neural models to obtain a GAM-like structure, and Wood [2017] realize feature shapes via penalized regression splines. The latter approach is of particular interest since it is an immediate extension of linear regression that inherits important theoretical results that are useful for our purpose.

A *regression spline* function of order q is a piecewise polynomial function obtained by dividing the domain of the function into contiguous intervals, and representing the function by a separate polynomial of order q in each interval. The points where the piecewise polynomial connect are known as knots, and the pieces are connected in such a way that the derivatives of the spline exist at the knots, i.e., with respect to derivatives a spline behaves similar to an ordinary polynomial of degree q over its entire domain. In the context of smoothing, one usually restricts attention to cubic splines.

---

[1]For the purpose of this exposition we say that a GAM is interpretable if all feature shapes can be visualized in two dimensions.

A key advantage of the spline approach is the fact that each spline function f_k can be represented as a linear combination of so called *base functions* b_j:

$$f_k(\cdot) = \sum_{j=1}^{d} \beta_j b_j(\cdot) = \mathbf{b}(\cdot)\boldsymbol{\beta}, \qquad\qquad (A.1)$$

where $\mathbf{b}(\cdot) = [b_1(\cdot), b_2(\cdot), \ldots, b_d(\cdot)]$, and $\boldsymbol{\beta} = [\beta_1, \beta_2, \ldots, \beta_d]^\top$.

The base functions are known in advance, and in order to fit a spline to data, one has to choose appropriate weights β_j. Conceptually, this is very similar to expressing a vector in a vector space explicitly in terms of a basis. In order to incorporate a spline in a model, one only has to substitute the basis representation in the GAM definition (bivariate functions are dropped for notational convenience):

$$g(\mathbb{E}[Y|\mathbf{x}]) = \sum_{k=1}^{p} \sum_{j=1}^{d_k} \beta_{kj} b_{kj}(x_k).$$

It is easy to see that splines are in essence linear smoothers, and that a GAM is in essence a linear model for the regressors $b_{kj}(x_k)$, $k = 1, \ldots, p$, $j = 1, \ldots, d_k$, which are nonlinear functions themselves. Note that only the composed feature shape is interpretable and not the individual β_{kj} or the base functions b_{kj}.

A.1.2   EXAMPLE

We consider a GAM for $n = 1, \ldots, N$ data points, using the same piecewise cubic spline functions for two features $k = 1, 2$. Following Hastie and Tibshirani [1990], the base functions for knots ξ_i, $i = 1, \ldots, I$ can be defined as follows:

$$
\begin{aligned}
b_{k1}(x_k^n) &= 1, \\
b_{k2}(x_k^n) &= x_k^n, \\
b_{k3}(x_k^n) &= (x_k^n)^2, \\
b_{k4}(x_k^n) &= (x_k^n)^3, \\
b_{ki}(x_k^n) &= (x_k^n - \xi_i)_+^3, \quad i = 1, \ldots, I,
\end{aligned}
$$

where $(a)_+ := \max(a, 0)$.

For a Gaussian response variable Y^n, two input features x_1 and x_2, and the identity link function, the GAM takes the following form:

$$Y^n = \beta_{11} + \beta_{12}x_1^n + \beta_{13}(x_1^n)^2 + \beta_{14}(x_1^n)^3 + \sum_{i=1}^{I} \beta_{1(i+4)}(x_1^n - \xi_i)_+^3$$

$$+ \beta_{21} + \beta_{22}x_2^n + \beta_{23}(x_2^n)^2 + \beta_{24}(x_2^n)^3 + \sum_{i=1}^{I} \beta_{2(i+4)}(x_2^n - \xi_i)_+^3$$

$$+ \epsilon^n$$

$$= \mathbf{G}^n \boldsymbol{\beta} + \epsilon^n,$$

where $\epsilon^n \sim \mathcal{N}(0, \sigma^2)$,

$$\mathbf{G}^n = \begin{bmatrix} b_{11}(x_1^n) & b_{12}(x_1^n) & \cdots & b_{1(I+4)}(x_1^n) & b_{21}(x_2^n) & b_{22}(x_2^n) & \cdots & b_{2(I+4)}(x_2^n) \end{bmatrix},$$

and

$$\boldsymbol{\beta} = \begin{bmatrix} \beta_{11} \\ \beta_{12} \\ \cdots \\ \beta_{1(I+4)} \\ \beta_{21} \\ \beta_{22} \\ \cdots \\ \beta_{2(I+4)} \end{bmatrix}.$$

The design matrix for the full dataset is written as

$$\begin{bmatrix} Y^1 \\ Y^2 \\ \vdots \\ Y^N \end{bmatrix} = \begin{bmatrix} \mathbf{G}^1 \\ \mathbf{G}^2 \\ \vdots \\ \mathbf{G}^N \end{bmatrix} \boldsymbol{\beta} + \begin{bmatrix} \epsilon^1 \\ \epsilon^2 \\ \vdots \\ \epsilon^N \end{bmatrix},$$

or, equivalently, as

$$\mathbf{Y} = \mathbf{G}\boldsymbol{\beta} + \boldsymbol{\epsilon}.$$

A.1.3   PARAMETER ESTIMATION

Consider following functional minimization problem, involving a general model h which is a twice differentiable function of a single covariate x for N datapoints:

$$\min_{h \in \mathfrak{H}} \sum_{n=1}^{N} (y^n - h(x^n))^2 + \lambda \int (h''(x))^2 dx,$$

where $\lambda \in \mathbb{R}^+$ and $\int (h''(x))^2 dx$ is a measure for the smoothness of a function over its domain—the wigglier the function the larger this quantity becomes. It turns out that the cubic spline function with a natural spline base is the unique minimizer of this problem. This corresponds essentially to cubic splines with a knot placed at each data point, thus yielding N base functions in the notation of Equation (A.1). Parameter estimation can be performed by penalized least squares estimation (PLSE) for the following optimization problem:

$$\hat{\boldsymbol{\beta}} = \underset{\boldsymbol{\beta} \in \mathbb{R}^s}{\text{argmin}} \|\mathbf{Y} - \mathbf{G}\boldsymbol{\beta}\|^2 + \sum_{k=1}^{p} \lambda_k \int (f_k''(x))^2 dx,$$

where $s = \sum_{k=1}^{p} d_k$ and $\lambda_k \in \mathbb{R}^+$ are tuning parameters that determine the weight of the smoothness penalties for the individual feature shapes and $\mathbf{G}$ is the basis matrix. Given data $\{(x^n, y^n)\}_{n=1}^{N}$, for a model with a single covariate and natural splines, $\mathbf{G}$ has the form of an $N \times N$ matrix

$$\mathbf{G} := [b_j(x^n)]_{j,n=1,\dots,N},$$

and the smoothness is measured by

$$\int (f''(x))^2 dx = \boldsymbol{\beta}^\top \boldsymbol{\Omega} \boldsymbol{\beta}.$$

The $N \times N$-matrix $\boldsymbol{\Omega}$ is called the penalty matrix and defined as

$$\boldsymbol{\Omega} := [\int b_s''(x)b_t''(x)dx]_{s,t=1,\dots,N}.$$

This reduces the minimization problem to the following form (note that λ is a scalar for the single covariate in our example):

$$\min_{\boldsymbol{\beta} \in \mathbb{R}^N} \|\mathbf{Y} - \mathbf{G}\boldsymbol{\beta}\|^2 + \lambda \boldsymbol{\beta}^\top \boldsymbol{\Omega} \boldsymbol{\beta}.$$

Given the similarity of this objective function to the one that arises in ordinary least squares regression, it is no surprise that the PLSE estimator for this problem is

$$\hat{\boldsymbol{\beta}} = (\mathbf{G}^\top \mathbf{G} + \lambda \boldsymbol{\Omega})^{-1} \mathbf{G}^\top \mathbf{y}.$$

Thus, by Equation (A.1), the estimated feature shape is

$$\hat{f}(\cdot) = \mathbf{b}(\cdot)(\mathbf{G}^\top \mathbf{G} + \lambda \boldsymbol{\Omega})^{-1} \mathbf{G}^\top \mathbf{y}.$$

One can see that the actual solution depends crucially on the choice of λ. Larger values for λ penalize functions with a lot of curvature dramatically, so that the final solution will be very

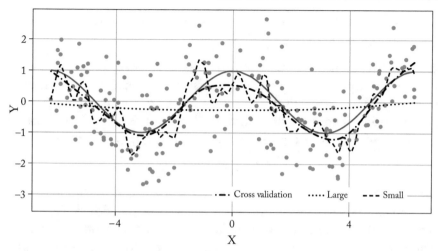

Figure A.1: This plot shows the data and fitted splines for a simulated toy example. The data were generated according to $Y = \cos(X) + \epsilon$ where $\epsilon \sim \mathcal{N}(0, 1)$. The points display the sampled data points ($n = 200$) and the red solid line the true $\mathbb{E}[Y|X]$. The dashdotted line is the estimated spline when λ was chosen by cross validation. We see that this estimator resembles the truth very closely, even for this very noisy data. The dotted line displays the estimated spline when λ is thousand times larger than the cross validated one. We see that this spline is more or less constantly zero, a result we would have obtained if we had applied ordinary linear regression to analyze this data. On the other hand, if we choose λ a thousand times smaller, than the estimated spline (dotted line) seems to follow the general pattern but is heavily shaped by erratic patterns in the data.

similar to a line. On the other hand, if λ is chosen too small, the resulting spline will accurately follow the datapoints. The result is a wiggly function that heavily overfits the data. An illustrative example for this is given in Figure A.1.

Furthermore, the actual model degrees of freedom are controlled by λ. Thus, instead of simply counting the number of free parameters defined by the architecture of a GAM, one computes *effective degrees of freedom* by taking the trace of the PLSE estimator (see Wood [2003]).

Estimation methods for the value for λ are cross validation [Wood, 2017], or marginal likelihood estimation, in tandem with estimation of $\boldsymbol{\beta}$ [Wood et al., 2016]. For a deeper treatment of smoothers and estimation of GAMs, see Hastie and Tibshirani [1990] and Wood [2017].

A.2   LINEAR MIXED EFFECTS MODELS

A.2.1   GENERAL FORM OF MODEL

A linear mixed effects model (LMEM) is an extension of a standard linear model that allows a rich linear structure in the random component of the model, where effects other than those that can be observed exhaustively (so-called *fixed effects*) are treated as a random samples from a larger population of normally distributed random variables (so-called *random effects*).

Given a dataset of N input-output pairs $\{(\mathbf{x}^n, y^n)\}_{n=1}^N$, the general form of an LMEM is

$$\mathbf{Y} = \mathbf{X}\boldsymbol{\beta} + \mathbf{Z}\mathbf{b} + \boldsymbol{\epsilon},$$

where $\mathbf{X}$ is an $(N \times k)$-matrix and $\mathbf{Z}$ is an $(N \times m)$-matrix, called model- or design-matrices (both are known), which relate the unobserved vectors $\boldsymbol{\beta}$ and $\mathbf{b}$ to $\mathbf{Y}$. $\boldsymbol{\beta}$ is a k-vector of fixed effects and $\mathbf{b}$ is an m-dimensional random vector called the random effects vector. $\boldsymbol{\epsilon}$ is an N-dimensional vector called the error component. The random vectors are assumed to have the following distributions:

$$\mathbf{b} \sim \mathcal{N}(0, \boldsymbol{\psi}_\theta),$$
$$\boldsymbol{\epsilon} \sim \mathcal{N}(0, \boldsymbol{\Lambda}_\theta),$$

where $\boldsymbol{\psi}_\theta$ and $\boldsymbol{\Lambda}_\theta$ are covariance matrices parameterized by the vector $\boldsymbol{\theta}$. The definition of an LMEM implies a definition of the distribution of the data vector $\mathbf{Y}$. In the context of the LMEM theory, we consider three important distributions, the first one of which is the distribution of $\mathbf{Y}|\mathbf{b}$. Obviously, when we fix $\mathbf{b}$, the only random component left is $\boldsymbol{\epsilon}$. Thus, the conditional distribution of $\mathbf{Y}$ given $\mathbf{b}$ is

$$\mathbf{Y}|\mathbf{b} \sim \mathcal{N}(\mathbf{X}\boldsymbol{\beta} + \mathbf{Z}\mathbf{b}, \boldsymbol{\Lambda}_\theta).$$

This distribution is the basis for the derivation of the so called mixed model equations or Henderson equations which provide estimators for the unknown quantities $\boldsymbol{\beta}$ and $\mathbf{b}$.

The second distribution of importance is the unconditional distribution of $\mathbf{Y}$. We defined $\mathbf{Y}$ to be a linear mapping of the independent zero mean Gaussian variables $\mathbf{b}$ and $\boldsymbol{\epsilon}$. Thus, $\mathbf{Y}$ is also a Gaussian with expected value $\mathbf{X}\boldsymbol{\beta}$. Since the variance can be written as $\mathbb{V}(\mathbf{Z}\mathbf{b}) = \mathbf{Z}\boldsymbol{\psi}_\theta \mathbf{Z}^\top$, we get

$$\mathbf{Y} \sim \mathcal{N}(\mathbf{X}\boldsymbol{\beta}, \mathbf{Z}\boldsymbol{\psi}_\theta \mathbf{Z}^\top + \boldsymbol{\Lambda}_\theta).$$

Note that $\mathbf{b}$ doesn't occur in this distribution, instead random effects enter the distribution only via the covariance matrix $\mathbf{Z}\boldsymbol{\psi}_\theta \mathbf{Z}^\top$. This reveals one of the main usages of mixed models, namely the convenient modelling of complex covariance structures when the data were not generated in the usual i.i.d. sampling fashion.

To complete our enumeration of important distributions, we derive the joint distribution of $\mathbf{b}$ and $\mathbf{Y}$. For this purpose, we simply stack $\mathbf{b}$ and $\mathbf{Y}$ together in a vector. Because both variables are multivariate Gaussians, the resulting vector is also a multivariate Gaussian, where the expected values as well as the block diagonal parts of the covariance matrix are inherited from $\mathbf{b}$ and $\mathbf{Y}$. Note that the covariance of $\mathbf{b}$ and $\mathbf{Y}$ is $\mathrm{Cov}(\mathbf{b}, \mathbf{Y}) = \boldsymbol{\psi_\theta} \mathbf{Z}^\top$ and let $\mathbf{V} = \mathbf{Z} \boldsymbol{\psi_\theta} \mathbf{Z}^\top + \boldsymbol{\Lambda_\theta}$, then

$$
\begin{bmatrix} \mathbf{b} \\ \mathbf{Y} \end{bmatrix} \sim \mathcal{N} \left(\begin{bmatrix} \mathbf{0} \\ \mathbf{X}\boldsymbol{\beta} \end{bmatrix}, \begin{bmatrix} \boldsymbol{\psi_\theta} & \boldsymbol{\psi_\theta} \mathbf{Z}^\top \\ \mathbf{Z}\boldsymbol{\psi_\theta} & \mathbf{V} \end{bmatrix} \right).
$$

Finally, let us say some words on the usage of LMEMs. As already mentioned, the most common application of LMEMs is to model complex covariance structures in the data when the usual i.i.d. assumptions fail to be applicable. This is the case, for example, for repeated or grouped, and thus non-independent, measurements. In this case, LMEMs provide a neat means to provide correct statistical inference about fixed effects (which is usually of primary interest to the analyst). Like other linear models, they can also be used to predict outcomes when the covariates are known. This prediction can be based on the unconditional distribution of $\mathbf{Y}$ or, when then random effects are also known, on the conditional distribution $\mathbf{Y}|\mathbf{b}$. Predictions based on the latter are usually associated with a smaller prediction uncertainty (via different covariance matrices). Furthermore, very much like Bayesian or other generative models, LMEMs can be used to generate synthetic data. A special case of LMEMs are models where $\mathbf{X} = \mathbf{0}$ and which therefore do not contain fixed effects. These models are called random effect models or variance component models. Their purpose is to partition the total observed variance of the outcome according to different sources. One application of these models are reliability studies.

A.2.2   EXAMPLE

Let us illustrate an LMEM by setting up a model for the analysis of the data in the hypothetical "lexical decision" experiment of Barr et al. [2013]. In this experiment four strings of characters were presented to four human subjects which had to decide whether or not the string forms an English word. The time from stimulus presentation to subject response (henceforth response time) was measured. The strings belong to two categories which are assumed to have an impact on the response time. For simplicity let us assume that string 1 and 2 belong to category A, and strings 3 and 4 to category B. The experiment was carried out to test this assumption.

For the analysis of these data one has to build a statistical model incorporating the variables of interest. The most basic model we could start with is

$$
y_{si} = \beta_0 + \beta_1 x_i + \epsilon_{si},
$$

where y_{si} denotes the response time of subject s for character string i, x_i encodes the category of character string i (where 0 represents category A and 1 category B), and $\epsilon_{si} \overset{iid}{\sim} \mathcal{N}(0, \sigma_{error}^2)$ is a random error component. The parameter β_0 is called the intercept. A simple calculation shows that $\beta_0 = \mathbb{E}[Y | x_i = 0]$ is the expected response time for items of category A. The parameter β_1 is called slope, and again a similar calculation shows that $\beta_1 = \mathbb{E}[Y | x_i = 1] - \mathbb{E}[Y | x_i = 0]$. It represents a measure of the difference of the expected response time for strings of category B versus strings of category A, and thus is the main quantity of interest for the analysis of this experiment.

As Barr points out, this model can not be a correct representation for the data generating mechanism of our experiment. A careful reading of the model definition reveals that we have assumed an error component that is independent of the measurements, which implies that the observations y_i are independent of each other. Obviously, the experimental setup violates this implication because we take repeated measurements from subjects and strings. Furthermore, the actual subjects and strings used in our experiment are just samples from larger populations, and we are not really interested in obtaining a fixed effect-like estimate for the expected response time of subject s or item i (nor is it possibly to do so with the data collected in this experiment). But we can account for the repeated measurements by incorporating appropriate random effects to model the covariance between measurements. In order to specify the structure of the random effects, Barr argues that it is reasonable to assume that there exist individual differences between subjects when processing strings from category A and B, and that these differences can be different for both categories. He also argues that some strings can be processed faster than others. Therefore, he proposes the following model

$$y_{si} = \beta_0 + b_s^{subject} + b_i^{item} + (\beta_1 + b_s^{slope})x_i + \epsilon_{si},$$

where the symbols used in the simpler model retain their meaning, and $b_s^{subject}$ is a random variable that represents the idiosyncratic deviation of subject s from β_0 (the overall expected response time for strings of category B), and b_i^{item} represent item specific deviations from this expectation. These two random variables modify the intercept of the model and are therefore called random intercepts in the mixed models literature. The random variable b_s^{slope} is the subject specific deviation from the global slope β_1 and is called a random slope. All the b are random variables, so we need to specify a the distribution for them. Let $\mathbf{b}_{si} := (b_s^{subject}, b_s^{slope}, b_i^{item})^\top$, then following Barr, we define

$$\mathbf{b}_{si} \overset{iid}{\sim} \mathcal{N}\left(\mathbf{0}, \begin{bmatrix} \sigma^2_{subject} & \sigma_{subject,\,slope} & 0 \\ \sigma_{subject,\,slope} & \sigma^2_{slope} & 0 \\ 0 & 0 & \sigma^2_{item} \end{bmatrix}\right),$$

where $\sigma^2_{subject}$, σ^2_{slope}, and σ^2_{item} are the respective variances of the random variables, and $\sigma_{subject,\,slope}$ denotes the covariance of the two random effects for each subject.

Let us proceed to write the complete model for the experimental data so that we can see how $\mathbf{X}$, $\mathbf{Z}$, $\mathbf{\Lambda}_\theta$, $\mathbf{\psi}_\theta$, and θ actually look like. Let us start by stacking the four model equations for a subject s together

$$
\begin{bmatrix} y_{s1} \\ y_{s2} \\ y_{s3} \\ y_{s4} \end{bmatrix} = \underbrace{\begin{bmatrix} 1 & 0 \\ 1 & 0 \\ 1 & 1 \\ 1 & 1 \end{bmatrix}}_{\mathbf{F}} \underbrace{\begin{bmatrix} \beta_0 \\ \beta_1 \end{bmatrix}}_{} + \underbrace{\begin{bmatrix} 1 & 0 \\ 1 & 0 \\ 1 & 1 \\ 1 & 1 \end{bmatrix}}_{\mathbf{S}} \underbrace{\begin{bmatrix} 1 & 0 & 0 & 0 \\ 0 & 1 & 0 & 0 \\ 0 & 0 & 1 & 0 \\ 0 & 0 & 0 & 1 \end{bmatrix}}_{\mathbf{I}} \begin{bmatrix} b_s^{subject} \\ b_s^{slope} \\ \cdots \\ b_1^{item} \\ b_2^{item} \\ b_3^{item} \\ b_4^{item} \end{bmatrix} + \underbrace{\begin{bmatrix} \epsilon_{s1} \\ \epsilon_{s2} \\ \epsilon_{s3} \\ \epsilon_{s4} \end{bmatrix}}_{\epsilon_s} .
$$

The matrix $\mathbf{F}$ encodes presence or absence of the fixed effects β_0 and β_1 in the equations. Its first column corresponds to the intercept, which is present in all of the four equations, and thus it contains only 1s. The second column is associated with the slope, which is only present when the items belong to category B. The second term on the right-hand side represents the random effects. The first two random effects $b_s^{subject}$ and b_s^{slope} are subject specific and their presence in the model equations is given by $\mathbf{S}$. Recall that $b_s^{subject}$ is a random intercept and b_s^{slope} a random slope, specific for subject s. The second block of random effects concerns the items. Each equation belongs to one item, thus each has a unique item specific random intercept. This is ensured by the diagonal matrix $\mathbf{I}$.

For the final model, we have to put the four blocks for each subject together.

$$
\begin{bmatrix} \mathbf{y}_1 \\ \mathbf{y}_2 \\ \mathbf{y}_3 \\ \mathbf{y}_4 \end{bmatrix} = \underbrace{\begin{bmatrix} \mathbf{F} \\ \mathbf{F} \\ \mathbf{F} \\ \mathbf{F} \end{bmatrix}}_{\mathbf{X}} \underbrace{\begin{bmatrix} \beta_0 \\ \beta_1 \end{bmatrix}}_{\beta} + \underbrace{\begin{bmatrix} \mathbf{S} & 0 & 0 & 0 & \mathbf{I} \\ 0 & \mathbf{S} & 0 & 0 & \mathbf{I} \\ 0 & 0 & \mathbf{S} & 0 & \mathbf{I} \\ 0 & 0 & 0 & \mathbf{S} & \mathbf{I} \end{bmatrix}}_{\mathbf{Z}} \underbrace{\begin{bmatrix} b_1^{subject} \\ b_1^{slope} \\ \cdots \\ b_2^{subject} \\ b_2^{slope} \\ \cdots \\ b_3^{subject} \\ b_3^{slope} \\ \cdots \\ b_4^{subject} \\ b_4^{slope} \\ \cdots \\ b_1^{item} \\ b_2^{item} \\ b_3^{item} \\ b_4^{item} \end{bmatrix}}_{\mathbf{b}} + \underbrace{\begin{bmatrix} \epsilon_1 \\ \epsilon_2 \\ \epsilon_3 \\ \epsilon_4 \end{bmatrix}}_{\epsilon} .
$$

Because every subject has to respond to every item, the final fixed effect design matrix $\mathbf{X}$ is simply a stack of four $\mathbf{F}$ matrices. For the random effects, we have to assure that each subject receives its own intercept and slope parameter. Therefore, we have to extend the vector $\mathbf{b}$ and impose a block diagonal structure for the subject dependent random effects in the random effects design matrix. To finalize the design matrix for the random effects $\mathbf{Z}$, we have to extend each block-row with a diagonal matrix $\mathbf{I}$.

In order to complete the model, we need to specify the covariance matrix for the random effects $\boldsymbol{\psi_\theta}$ and the error component $\boldsymbol{\Lambda_\theta}$. When we look at $\mathbf{b}$, we see that it is composed of four subject specific blocks, each with a covariance matrix

$$\Sigma_\theta^{subject} := \left(\begin{bmatrix} \sigma_{subject}^2 & \sigma_{subject,\, slope} \\ \sigma_{subject,\, slope} & \sigma_{slope}^2 \end{bmatrix} \right),$$

and one block for the items. By design of the experiment, the items are generated (or drawn, in a probabilistic parlance) independent of each other. For the multivariate normal distribution, independence of components is equivalent to zero covariance between the components. Thus, the covariance matrix for the item block of $\mathbf{b}$ looks like

$$\Sigma_\theta^{item} := \begin{bmatrix} \sigma_{item}^2 & 0 & 0 & 0 \\ 0 & \sigma_{item}^2 & 0 & 0 \\ 0 & 0 & \sigma_{item}^2 & 0 \\ 0 & 0 & 0 & \sigma_{item}^2 \end{bmatrix}.$$

By design of the experiment, the subjects are also independent of each other, thus we can stack the individual covariance matrices together in a block diagonal fashion, yielding

$$\boldsymbol{\psi_\theta} = \begin{bmatrix} \Sigma_\theta^{subject} & 0 & 0 & 0 & 0 \\ 0 & \Sigma_\theta^{subject} & 0 & 0 & 0 \\ 0 & 0 & \Sigma_\theta^{subject} & 0 & 0 \\ 0 & 0 & 0 & \Sigma_\theta^{subject} & 0 \\ 0 & 0 & 0 & 0 & \Sigma_\theta^{item} \end{bmatrix}$$

as the covariance matrix for $\mathbf{b}$. The last model component we need to specify is the covariance matrix for $\boldsymbol{\epsilon}$. Recall that we had to introduce random effects in the model to ensure independence between observations, so that we can now make an i.i.d. assumption for ϵ_{si}. Consequently, the covariance matrix for the error component is

$$\boldsymbol{\Lambda_\theta} = \sigma_{error}^2 \begin{bmatrix} 1 & 0 & \cdots & 0 \\ 0 & 1 & \cdots & 0 \\ \vdots & \vdots & \ddots & \vdots \\ 0 & 0 & \cdots & 1 \end{bmatrix}.$$

A final look at all the covariance matrices show us that they are determined by the four terms $\sigma_{error}^2, \sigma_{subject}^2, \sigma_{slope}^2, \sigma_{item}^2$ and $\sigma_{subject,\, slope}$. Putting them together in a single parameter vector $\boldsymbol{\theta} = (\sigma_{error}^2, \sigma_{subject}^2, \sigma_{slope}^2, \sigma_{item}^2, \sigma_{subject,\, slope})^\top$ finalizes our description.

A.2.3 PARAMETER OPTIMIZATION

In principle there are two ways to calculate maximum likelihood estimators for an LMEM. First, we present a conceptually simple approach based on the distribution $p(\mathbf{Y}|\boldsymbol{\beta}, \boldsymbol{\theta})$. Let us assume that $\boldsymbol{\theta}$ is known, so that $\mathbf{V} = \mathbf{Z}\boldsymbol{\psi}_{\boldsymbol{\theta}}\mathbf{Z}^{\top} + \boldsymbol{\Lambda}_{\boldsymbol{\theta}}$ is known, then

$$p(\mathbf{Y}|\boldsymbol{\beta}, \boldsymbol{\theta}) = \frac{1}{\sqrt{|\mathbf{V}|(2\pi)^N}} \exp\left(-\frac{1}{2}(\mathbf{Y} - \mathbf{X}\boldsymbol{\beta})^{\top}\mathbf{V}^{-1}(\mathbf{Y} - \mathbf{X}\boldsymbol{\beta})\right).$$

The maximum likelihood estimator is found by optimizing the log-likelihood objective (terms and factors not involving $\boldsymbol{\beta}$ are dropped)

$$\ell(\boldsymbol{\beta}) = -\frac{1}{2}(\mathbf{Y} - \mathbf{X}\boldsymbol{\beta})^{\top}\mathbf{V}^{-1}(\mathbf{Y} - \mathbf{X}\boldsymbol{\beta}).$$

This is a simple convex optimization problem similar to the PLSE used for GAMs, with the solution

$$\hat{\boldsymbol{\beta}} = (\mathbf{X}^{\top}\mathbf{V}^{-1}\mathbf{X})^{-1}\mathbf{X}^{\top}\mathbf{V}^{-1}\mathbf{Y}.$$

If we want to obtain estimates (also called predictions) for the random effects, we estimate $\mathbb{E}_{\mathbf{b}|\mathbf{Y}=\mathbf{y}}[\mathbf{b}]$. Recall that the joint distribution of $\mathbf{b}$ and $\mathbf{Y}$ is

$$\begin{bmatrix} \mathbf{b} \\ \mathbf{Y} \end{bmatrix} \sim \mathcal{N}\left(\begin{bmatrix} \mathbf{0} \\ \mathbf{X}\boldsymbol{\beta} \end{bmatrix}, \begin{bmatrix} \boldsymbol{\psi}_{\boldsymbol{\theta}} & \boldsymbol{\psi}_{\boldsymbol{\theta}}\mathbf{Z}^{\top} \\ \mathbf{Z}\boldsymbol{\psi}_{\boldsymbol{\theta}} & \mathbf{V} \end{bmatrix}\right),$$

which yields for the conditional expectation of $\mathbf{b}$ given $\mathbf{Y} = \mathbf{y}$, by definition of the conditional expectation of multivariate Gaussians, the following expression:

$$\mathbb{E}_{\mathbf{b}|\mathbf{Y}=\mathbf{y}}[\mathbf{b}] = (\boldsymbol{\psi}_{\boldsymbol{\theta}}\mathbf{Z}^{\top}\mathbf{V}^{-1})(\mathbf{Y} - \mathbf{X}\boldsymbol{\beta}).$$

Substituting $\hat{\boldsymbol{\beta}}$ for $\boldsymbol{\beta}$ we obtain the following estimator for $\mathbf{b}$:

$$\hat{\mathbf{b}} = (\boldsymbol{\psi}_{\boldsymbol{\theta}}\mathbf{Z}^{\top}\mathbf{V}^{-1})(\mathbf{Y} - \mathbf{X}\hat{\boldsymbol{\beta}}).$$

The estimated values obtained via the approach given above are identical to the estimates of a more complex estimator called the Henderson equations (or mixed model equations, see Henderson et al. [1959]). They are based on the distribution $p(\mathbf{Y}|\mathbf{b}, \boldsymbol{\beta}, \boldsymbol{\theta})$ and allow estimating $\boldsymbol{\beta}$ and $\mathbf{b}$ simultaneously, and assume in general that $\boldsymbol{\theta}$ is unknown. The advantage of the Henderson equations is that they allow a computationally more efficient estimation since only the inversion of matrices of much smaller dimension than $\mathbf{V}$ is required. In general, when $\boldsymbol{\theta}$ is unknown, it needs to be replaced by an estimator. There are a variety of different techniques to do so, and the inclined reader is referred to Demidenko [2013], McCulloch and Searle [2001], Pinheiro and Bates [2000], West et al. [2007], and Wood [2017] for an extensive elaboration of these.

A.3   THE DISTRIBUTION OF THE LIKELIHOOD RATIO STATISTIC

A.3.1   SCORE FUNCTION AND FISHER INFORMATION

A key concept in likelihood-based statistical methods is the *score function*. Let Y be a random variable distributed according to $p_\theta(y)$, and let $\ell(\theta) := \log p_\theta(y)$. Then the score function is defined as

$$S(\theta) := \frac{\partial}{\partial \theta} \ell(\theta).$$

The maximum likelihood estimator $\hat{\theta}$ is thus the solution to the *score equation* which is defined as

$$S(\theta = \hat{\theta}) = 0. \tag{A.2}$$

The *Fisher information* $I(\theta)$ of Y is defined as

$$I(\theta) := \mathbb{E}_\theta[S(\theta)^2] = \int S(\theta)^2 p_\theta(y) dy. \tag{A.3}$$

Under the mild assumption that the order of integration and differentiation can be reversed, $I(\theta)$ can be written as the variance of the score function:

$$I(\theta) := \mathbb{V}_\theta[S(\theta)]. \tag{A.4}$$

This can be shown by the following calculations:

$$\begin{aligned}
\mathbb{E}_\theta[S(\theta)] &= \mathbb{E}\left[\frac{\partial}{\partial \theta} \ell(\theta)\right] \\
&= \int \left[\frac{\partial}{\partial \theta} \ell(\theta)\right] p_\theta(y) dy \\
&= \int \left[\frac{\partial}{\partial \theta} \log p_\theta(y)\right] p_\theta(y) dy \\
&= \int \left[\frac{\frac{\partial}{\partial \theta} p_\theta(y)}{p_\theta(y)}\right] p_\theta(y) dy \\
&= \frac{\partial}{\partial \theta} \int p_\theta(y) dy \\
&= \frac{\partial}{\partial \theta} 1 = 0.
\end{aligned}$$

The equivalence of Equations (A.4) and (A.3) follows since

$$\begin{aligned}
\mathbb{V}_\theta[S(\theta)] &= \mathbb{E}_\theta[S(\theta)^2] - \mathbb{E}_\theta[S(\theta)]^2 \\
&= \mathbb{E}_\theta[S(\theta)^2] - 0.
\end{aligned}$$

Given that $\ell(\theta) := \log p_\theta(y)$ is twice differentiable in θ, another useful equivalence of $I(\theta)$ can be shown:

$$I(\theta) = -\mathbb{E}_\theta \left[\frac{\partial^2}{\partial \theta^2} \ell(\theta) \right]. \tag{A.5}$$

The second derivative of $\ell(\theta)$ is

$$\frac{\partial^2}{\partial \theta^2} \ell(\theta) = \frac{\partial^2}{\partial \theta^2} \log p_\theta(y)$$

$$= \frac{p_\theta(y) \frac{\partial^2}{\partial \theta^2} p_\theta(y) - \left[\frac{\partial}{\partial \theta} p_\theta(y) \right]^2}{[p_\theta(y)]^2}$$

$$= \frac{\frac{\partial^2}{\partial \theta^2} p_\theta(y)}{p_\theta(y)} - \left[\frac{\partial}{\partial \theta} \ell(\theta) \right]^2$$

$$= \frac{\frac{\partial^2}{\partial \theta^2} p_\theta(y)}{p_\theta(y)} - [S(\theta)]^2 .$$

Taking expectations and assuming that the order of integration and differentiation can be reversed, we see that first term cancels, and we end up with an equivalence of Equations (A.5) and (A.3):

$$\mathbb{E}_\theta \left[\frac{\partial^2}{\partial \theta^2} \ell(\theta) \right] = \int \left[\frac{\partial^2}{\partial \theta^2} p_\theta(y) \right] dy - I(\theta)$$

$$= 0 - I(\theta).$$

A.3.2   TAYLOR EXPANSION AND ASYMPTOTIC DISTRIBUTION

Assume $\theta_0, \hat{\theta} \in \mathbb{R}$ to be scalars indicating our null hypothesis and alternative hypothesis, respectively. Furthermore, assume a random variable Y with distribution $p_\theta(y)$, as above. The likelihood ratio statistic can then be written as follows:

$$W = -2 \log \Lambda = -2 \log \frac{p_{\theta_0}(y)}{p_{\hat{\theta}}(y)} = 2 \left(\ell(\hat{\theta}) - \ell(\theta_0) \right).$$

The central argument employed in Wilks [1938] is to replace $\ell(\theta_0)$ by its quadratic Taylor expansion around the maximum likelihood estimator $\hat{\theta}$. Let us first consider the case of a single observed sample point:

$$W = 2 \left(\ell(\hat{\theta}) - \ell(\theta_0) \right)$$

$$\approx 2 \left(\ell(\hat{\theta}) - \ell(\hat{\theta}) - (\theta_0 - \hat{\theta}) \frac{\partial}{\partial \theta} \ell(\hat{\theta}) - \frac{1}{2} (\theta_0 - \hat{\theta})^2 \frac{\partial^2}{\partial \theta^2} \ell(\hat{\theta}) \right)$$

$$= (\hat{\theta} - \theta_0)^2 \frac{\partial^2}{\partial \theta^2} \ell(\hat{\theta}).$$

The result follows by the score Equation (A.2). For N i.i.d observations, $\ell(\hat{\theta}_N) = \sum_{n=1}^{N} \ell_{y_i}(\hat{\theta}_N) := \sum_{n=1}^{N} \log p_{\hat{\theta}_N}(y_i)$. Hence, we get the following approximation:

$$W \approx (\hat{\theta}_N - \theta_0)^2 \sum_{n=1}^{N} \frac{\partial^2}{\partial \theta^2} \ell_{y_i}(\hat{\theta}_N)$$

$$= \left(\sqrt{N}(\hat{\theta}_N - \theta_0)\right)^2 \left(\frac{1}{N} \sum_{n=1}^{N} \frac{\partial^2}{\partial \theta^2} \ell_{y_i}(\hat{\theta}_N)\right)$$

$$\xrightarrow[n \to \infty]{p} \left(\sqrt{N}(\hat{\theta}_N - \theta_0)\right)^2 I(\theta_0).$$

The result follows since the empirical Fisher information converges in probability to the Fisher Information Matrix $I(\theta_0)$. An application of Theorem 4.5 then lets us state the asymptotic distribution of the likelihood ratio statistic as follows:

$$W \overset{app}{\sim} \chi^2_{df=1}.$$

For more information on likelihood-based statistical methods and related asymptotic results, the reader is referred to Davison [2003], Pawitan [2001], and van der Vaart [1998].

Bibliography

Agarwal, R., Frosst, N., Zhang, X., Caruana, R., and Hinton, G. E. (2020). Neural additive models: Interpretable machine learning with neural nets. In *Proc. of the ICML Workshop on Human Interpretability in Machine Learning*. 31, 115

Agrawal, A., Batra, D., Parikh, D., and Kembhavi, A. (2018). Don't just assume; look and answer: Overcoming priors for visual question answering. In *Proc. of the IEEE Conference on Computer Vision and Pattern Recognition (CVPR)*, Salt Lake City, UT. DOI: 10.1109/cvpr.2018.00522 9, 10

Agresti, A. (2002). *Categorical Data Analysis*. Wiley. DOI: 10.1002/0471249688 25

Alvarez-Melis, D. and Jaakkola, T. S. (2018). Towards robust interpretability with self-explaining neural networks. In *Proc. of the 32nd Conference on Neural Information Processing Systems (NeurIPS)*, Montreal, Canada. 17

Amodio, S., Aria, M., and D'Ambrosio, A. (2014). On concurvity in nonlinear and non-parameric regression models. *Statistica*, 1:85–98. DOI: 10.6092/issn.1973-2201/4599 17

Andrews, D. W. (2000). Inconsistency of the bootstrap when a parameter is on the boundary of the parameter space. *Econometrica*, 68(2):399–405. DOI: 10.1111/1468-0262.00114 65

Arjovsky, M., Bottou, L., Gulrajani, I., and Lopez-Paz, D. (2019). Invariant risk minimization. *CoRR*. 1, 2, 20, 25

Artstein, R. and Poesio, M. (2008). Inter-coder agreement for computational linguistics. *Computational Linguistics*, 34(4):555–596. DOI: 10.1162/coli.07-034-r2 57

Baayen, R., Davidson, D., and Bates, D. (2008). Mixed-effects modeling with crossed random effects for subjects and items. *Journal of Memory and Language*, 59:390–412. DOI: 10.1016/j.jml.2007.12.005 68

Bahdanau, D., Cho, K., and Bengio, Y. (2015). Neural machine translation by jointly learning to align and translate. In *Proc. of the International Conference on Learning Representations (ICLR)*, San Diego, CA. 82

Balzer, W. (1992). The structuralist view of measurement: An extension of received measurement theories. In Savage, C. and Ehrlich, P., Eds., *Philosophical and Foundational Issues in Measurement Theory*, pages 93–117, Erlbaum. DOI: 10.4324/9780203772256-10 15, 16, 17

Balzer, W. and Brendel, K. R. (2019). *Theorie der Wissenschaften*. Springer. DOI: 10.1007/978-3-658-21222-3 4, 15, 16, 28

Barr, D. J., Levy, R., Scheepers, C., and Tilly, H. J. (2013). Random effects structure for confirmatory hypothesis testing: Keep it maximal. *Journal of Memory and Language*, 68(3):255–278. DOI: 10.1016/j.jml.2012.11.001 68, 112, 121

Barrault, L., Biesialska, M., Bojar, O., Costa-jussà, M. R., Federmann, C., Graham, Y., Grundkiewicz, R., Haddow, B., Huck, M., Joanis, E., Kocmi, T., Koehn, P., Lo, C.-k., Ljubešić, N., Monz, C., Morishita, M., Nagata, M., Nakazawa, T., Pal, S., Post, M., and Zampieri, M. (2020). Findings of the 2020 conference on machine translation (WMT20). In *Proc. of the 5th Conference on Machine Translation (WMT)*. 88

Bates, D., Mächler, M., Bolker, B. M., and Walker, S. C. (2015). Fitting linear mixed-effects models using lme4. *Journal of Statistical Software*, 67(1):1–48. DOI: 10.18637/jss.v067.i01 68, 89

Bates, S., Hastie, T., and Tibshirani, R. (2021). Cross-validation: What does it estimate and how well does it do it? *CoRR*. 65

Bengio, Y. and Grandvalet, Y. (2004). No unbiased estimator of the variance of k-fold cross-validation. *Journal of Machine Learning Research*, 5:1089–1105. 65

Bentivogli, L., Bertoldi, N., Cettolo, M., Federico, M., Negri, M., and Turchi, M. (2016). On the evaluation of adaptive machine translation for human post-editing. *IEEE Transactions on Audio, Speech, and Language Processing (TASLP)*, 24(2):388–399. DOI: 10.1109/taslp.2015.2509241 66

Berg-Kirkpatrick, T., Burkett, D., and Klein, D. (2012). An empirical investigation of statistical significance in NLP. In *Proc. of the Joint Conference on Empirical Methods in Natural Language Processing and Computational Natural Language Learning (EMNLP-CoNLL)*, Jeju Island, Korea. 99

Bergstra, J. and Bengio, Y. (2012). Random search for hyper-parameter optimization. *Journal of Machine Learning Research (JMLR)*, 13:281–305. 79, 87

Bickel, P. J. and Freedman, D. A. (1981). Some asymptotic theory for the bootstrap. *The Annals of Statistics*, 9(6):1196–1217. DOI: 10.1214/aos/1176345637 65

Borsboom, D. (2005). *Measuring the Mind. Conceptual Issues in Contemporary Psychometrics*. Cambridge University Press. DOI: 10.1017/cbo9780511490026 12

Borsboom, D. and Mellenbergh, G. J. (2007). Test validity in cognitive assessment. In Leighton, J. P. and Gierl, M. J., Eds., *Cognitive Diagnostic Assessment for Education. Theory and Applications*, pages 85–115, Cambridge University Press. DOI: 10.1017/cbo9780511611186.004 12, 13

Borsboom, D., Mellenbergh, G. J., and van Heerden, J. (2004). The concept of validity. *Psychological Review*, 111(4):1061–1071. DOI: 10.1037/0033-295x.111.4.1061 4, 12, 13, 17, 20

Bottou, L., Curtis, F. E., and Nocedal, J. (2018). Optimization methods for large-scale machine learning. *SIAM Review*, 60(2):223–311. DOI: 10.1137/16m1080173 1

Bousquet, O., Boucheron, S., and Lugosi, G. (2004). Introduction to statistical learning theory. In Bousquet, O., von Luxburg, U., and Rätsch, G., Eds., *Advanced Lectures on Machine Learning*, pages 169–207, Springer, Berlin. DOI: 10.1007/978-3-540-28650-9_8 1

Bowman, S. R. and Dahl, G. (2021). What will it take to fix benchmarking in natural language understanding? In *Proc. of the Conference of the North American Chapter of the Association for Computational Linguistics: Human Language Technologies (NAACL-HLT)*. DOI: 10.18653/v1/2021.naacl-main.385 2

Brennan, R. L. (2001). *Generalizability Theory*. Springer. DOI: 10.1007/978-1-4757-3456-0 5, 66, 67, 68, 69, 70, 86, 87

Brin, S. and Page, L. (1998). The anatomy of a large-scale hypertextual web search engine. In *Proc. of the 7th International World-Wide Web Conference (WWW)*, Brisbane, Australia. DOI: 10.1016/s0169-7552(98)00110-x 33

Canty, A. J., Davison, A. C., Hinkley, D. V., and Ventura, V. (2006). Bootstrap diagnostics and remedies. *The Canadian Journal of Statistics*, 34(1):5–27. DOI: 10.1002/cjs.5550340103 65, 98, 99

Card, D., Henderson, P., Khandelwal, U., Jia, R., Mahowald, K., and Jurafsky, D. (2020). With little power comes great responsibility. In *Proc. of the Conference on Empirical Methods in Natural Language Processing (EMNLP)*. DOI: 10.18653/v1/2020.emnlp-main.745 113

Chapelle, O. and Chang, Y. (2011). Yahoo! learning to rank challenge overview. In *Proc. of the Yahoo! Learning to Rank Challenge*, Haifa, Israel. 32

Chen, X., Duan, Y., Houthooft, R., Schulman, J., Sutskever, I., and Abbeel, P. (2016). Infogan: Interpretable representation learning by information maximizing generative adversarial nets. In *Advances in Neural Information Processing Systems (NIPS)*, Barcelona, Spain. 18

Clark, C., Yatskar, M., and Zettlemoyer, L. (2019). Don't take the easy way out: Ensemble based methods for avoiding known dataset biases. In *Proc. of the Conference on Empirical Methods in Natural Language Processing and the 9th International Joint Conference on Natural Language Processing (EMNLP-IJCNLP)*, Hong Kong, China. DOI: 10.18653/v1/d19-1418 2, 10, 20, 25

Clark, J., Dyer, C., Lavie, A., and Smith, N. (2011). Better hypothesis testing for statistical machine translation: Controlling for optimizer instability. In *Proc. of the 49th Annual Meeting of the Association for Computational Linguistics (ACL)*, Portland, OR. 91, 101, 113

Cohen, J. (1960). A coefficient of agreement for nominal scales. *Educational and Psychological Measurement*, 20(1):37–46. DOI: 10.1177/001316446002000104 57

Cohen, P. R. (1995). *Empirical Methods for Artificial Intelligence*. The MIT Press. xv, 63, 65, 94, 99

Collins, M., Koehn, P., and Kučerová, I. (2005). Clause restructuring for statistical machine translation. In *Proc. of the 43rd Annual Meeting of the Association for Computational Linguistics (ACL)*, Ann Arbor, MI. DOI: 10.3115/1219840.1219906 91

Collobert, R., Weston, J., Michael Karlen, L. B., Kavukcuoglu, K., and Kuksa, P. (2011). Natural language processing (almost) from scratch. *Journal of Machine Learning Research*, 12:2461–2505. 18

Corfield, D., Schölkopf, B., and Vapnik, V. (2009). Falsificationism and statistical learning theory: Comparing the Popper and Vapnik-Chervonenkis dimensions. *Journal for General Philosophy of Science*, 40:51–58. DOI: 10.1007/s10838-009-9091-3 1

Cover, T. M. and Thomas, J. A. (1991). *Elements of Information Theory*. Wiley. DOI: 10.1002/0471200611 25

Cox, D. and Reid, N. (2000). *The Theory of the Design of Experiments*. Chapman & Hall/CRC. DOI: 10.1201/9781420035834 1

Cronbach, L. J. (1951). Coefficient alpha and the internal structure of tests. *Psychometrika*, 16(3):297–334. DOI: 10.1007/bf02310555 87

Cronbach, L. J. and Meehl, P. E. (1955). Construct validity in psychological tests. *Psychological Bulletin*, 52(4):281–302. DOI: 10.1037/h0040957 12

D'Amour, A., Heller, K. A., Moldovan, D., Adlam, B., Alipanahi, B., Beutel, A., Chen, C., Deaton, J., Eisenstein, J., Homan, M. D., Hormozdiari, F., Houlsby, N., Hou, S., Jerfel, G., Karthikesalingam, A., Lucic, M., Ma, Y., McLean, C. Y., Mincu, D., Mitani, A., Montanari, A., Nado, Z., Natarajan, V., Nielson, C., Osborne, T. F., Raman, R., Ramasamy, K., Sayres, R., Schrou, J., Seneviratne, M., Sequeira, S., Suresh, H., Veitch, V., Vladymyrov, M., Wang, X., Webster, K., Yadlowsky, S., Yun, T., Zhai, X., and Sculley, D. (2020). Underspecification presents challenges for credibility in modern machine learning. *ArXiv:2011.03395*. 89

Davison, A. C. (2003). *Statistical Models*. Cambridge University Press. DOI: 10.1017/cbo9780511815850 128 de Stoppelaar, S. F., van't Veer, C., and van der Poll, T. (2014). The role of platelets in sepsis. *Thrombosis and Haemostasis*, 112(4):666–667. DOI: 10.1160/th14-02-0126 52

DeGroot, M. H. and Schervish, M. J. (2012). *Probability and Statistics*, 4th ed., Addison-Wesley. 65, 108

Dellinger, R., Levy, M., Rhodes, A., Annane, D., Gerlach, H., Opal, S. M., Sevransky, J., Sprung, C., Douglas, I. S., Osborn, T. M., Jaeschke, R., Nunnally, M., Townsend, S., Reinhart, K., Kleinpell, R., Angus, D., Deutschman, C., Machado, F., Rubenfeld, G., Webb, S., Beale, R., Vincent, J., and Moreno, R. (2013). Surviving sepsis campaign: International guidelines for management of severe sepsis and septic shock: 2012. *Critical Care Medicine*, 41(2):580–637. DOI: 10.1097/CCM.0b013e31827e83af 11

Demidenko, E. (2013). *Mixed Models: Theory and Applications with R*. Wiley. 68, 89, 125

Devlin, J., Chang, M.-W., Lee, K., and Toutanova, K. (2019). BERT: Pre-training of deep bidirectional transformers for language understanding. In *Proc. of the Conference of the North American Chapter of the Association for Computational Linguistics: Human Language Technologies (NAACL:HLT)*, Minneapolis, MN. 18, 23

Dietterich, T. G. (1998). Approximate statistical tests for comparing supervised classification learning algorithms. *Neural Computation*, 10(7):1895–1924. DOI: 10.1162/089976698300017197 65

Ding, Y., Liu, Y., Luan, H., and Sun, M. (2017). Visualizing and understanding neural machine translation. In *Proc. of the 55th Annual Meeting of the Association for Computational Linguistics (ACL)*, Vancouver, Canada. DOI: 10.18653/v1/p17-1106 18

Dodge, J., Gururangan, S., Card, D., Schwartz, R., and Smith, N. A. (2019). Show your work: Improved reporting of experimental results. In *Proc. of the Conference on Empirical Methods in Natural Language Processing and the 9th International Joint Conference on Natural Language Processing (EMNLP-IJCNLP)*. DOI: 10.18653/v1/d19-1224 2, 63, 65, 74

Doshi-Velez, F. and Kim, B. (2017). Towards a rigorous science of interpretable machine learning. *CoRR*. 17

Dror, R., Baumer, G., Bogomolov, M., and Reichart, R. (2017). Replicability analysis for natural language processing: Testing significance with multiple datasets. In *Transactions of the Association for Computational Linguistics (TACL)*, 5:471–486. DOI: 10.1162/tacl_a_00074 56, 92, 112

Dror, R., Peled, L., Shlomov, S., and Reichart, R. (2020). *Statistical Significance Testing for Natural Language Processing*. Morgan & Claypool. DOI: 10.2200/s00994ed1v01y202002hlt045 3, 5, 91, 92, 97, 113

Dror, R., Shlomov, S., and Reichart, R. (2019). Deep dominance—how to properly compare deep neural models. In *Proc. of the 57th Annual Meeting of the Association for Computational Linguistics (ACL)*, Florence, Italy. DOI: 10.18653/v1/p19-1266 92, 112

Dyagilev, K. and Saria, S. (2016). Learning (predictive) risk scores in the presence of censoring due to interventions. *Machine Learning*, 20(3):323–348. DOI: 10.1007/s10994-015-5527-7 11

Efron, B. and Hastie, T. (2016). *Computer Age Statistical Inference. Algorithms, Evidence, and Data Science*. Cambridge University Press. DOI: 10.1017/cbo9781316576533 63

Efron, B. and Tibshirani, R. J. (1993). *An Introduction to the Bootstrap*. Chapman and Hall. DOI: 10.1007/978-1-4899-4541-9 57, 63, 65, 91, 97, 100

Ferro, N. and Silvello, G. (2016). A general linear mixed models approach to study system component effects. In *Proc. of the 39th International ACM SIGIR Conference on Research and Development in Information Retrieval*, Pisa, Italy. DOI: 10.1145/2911451.2911530 87

Fisher, R. A. (1925). *Statistical Methods for Research Workers*. Oliver and Boyd. 4, 5, 67, 69, 86

Fisher, R. A. (1935). *The Design of Experiments*. Hafner. 4, 91, 99, 113

Forde, J. Z. and Paganini, M. (2019). The scientific method in the science of machine learning. In *Proc. of the ICLR Debugging Machine Learning Models Workshop*, New Orleans, LA. 91

Gitelman, L., Ed. (2013). *Raw Data is an Oxymoron*. MIT Press. 17

Glorot, X., Bordes, A., and Bengio, Y. (2011). Deep sparse rectifier neural networks. In *Proc. of the 14th International Conference on Artificial Intelligence and Statistics (AISTATS)*, Fort Lauderdale, FL. 47, 76

Goodman, S. N., Fanelli, D., and Ioannidis, J. P. A. (2016). What does research reproducibility mean? *Science Transactions on Medicine*, 8(341):1–6. DOI: 10.1126/scitranslmed.aaf5027 56

Gorman, K. and Bedrick, S. (2019). We need to talk about standard splits. In *Proc. of the 57th Annual Meeting of the Association for Computational Linguistics (ACL)*, Florence, Italy. DOI: 10.18653/v1/p19-1267 11

Graf, E. and Azzopardi, L. (2008). A methodology for building a patent test collection for prior art search. In *Proc. of the 2nd International Workshop on Evaluating Information Access (EVIA)*, pages 60–71, Tokyo, Japan. 4, 11, 32

Graham, Y., Mathur, N., and Baldwin, T. (2014). Randomized significance tests in machine translation. In *Proc. of the 9th Workshop on Statistical Machine Translation (WMT)*, Baltimore, MD. DOI: 10.3115/v1/w14-3333 91

Green, S., Wang, S. I., Chuang, J., Heer, J., Schuster, S., and Manning, C. D. (2014). Human effort and machine learnability in computer aided translation. In *Proc. the Conference on Empirical Methods in Natural Language Processing (EMNLP)*, Doha, Qatar. DOI: 10.3115/v1/d14-1130 66

Guo, Y. and Gomes, C. (2009). Ranking structured documents: A large margin based approach for patent prior art search. In *Proc. of the International Joint Conference on Artificial Intelligence (IJCAI)*, pages 1058–1064, Pasadena, CA. 4, 11, 32

Gururangan, S., Swayamdipta, S., Levy, O., Schwartz, R., Bowman, S., and Smith, N. A. (2018). Annotation artifacts in natural language inference data. In *Proc. of the Conference of the North American Chapter of the Association for Computational Linguistics: Human Language Technologies (NAACL-HLT)*, New Orleans, LA. DOI: 10.18653/v1/n18-2017 9, 10

Habelitz, P. and Keuper, J. (2020). PHS: A toolbox for parallel hyperparameter search. *CoRR*. 88

Hallgren, K. A. (2012). Computing inter-rater reliability for observational data: An overview and tutorial. *Tutorials in Quantitative Methods for Psychology*, 8(1):23–34. DOI: 10.20982/tqmp.08.1.p023 55

Hardt, M. and Recht, B. (2021). Patterns, predictions, and actions: A story about machine learning. https://mlstory.org xv

Hastie, T. and Tibshirani, R. (1986). Generalized additive models. *Statistical Science*, 1(3):297–318. DOI: 10.1214/ss/1177013604 30

Hastie, T. and Tibshirani, R. (1990). *Generalized Additive Models*. Chapman and Hall. DOI: 0.1201/9780203753781 29, 31, 115, 116, 119

Hastie, T., Tibshirani, R., and Friedman, J. (2001). *The Elements of Statistical Learning. Data Mining, Inference, and Prediction*. Springer. DOI: 10.1007/978-0-387-84858-7 97

Heckman, N. E. (1986). Spline smoothing in a partly linear model. *Journal of the Royal Statistical Society B*, 48(2):244–248. DOI: 10.1111/j.2517-6161.1986.tb01407.x 31

Henderson, C., Kempthorne, O., Searle, S., and von Krosigk, C. (1959). The estimation of environmental and genetic trends from records subject to culling. *Biometrics*, 15(2):192–218. DOI: 10.2307/2527669 125

Henderson, P., Islam, R., Bachmann, P., Pineau, J., Precup, D., and Meger, D. (2018). Deep reinforcement learning that matters. In *Proc. of the 32nd AAAI Conference on Artificial Intelligence (AAAI)*, New Orleans, LA. 2, 62, 63, 75, 92

Henry, K. E., Hager, D. N., Pronovost, P. J., and Saria, S. (2015). A targeted real-time early warning score (TREWScore) for septic shock. *Science Translational Medicine*, 7(229):1–9. DOI: 10.1126/scitranslmed.aab3719 11

Higgins, I., Matthey, L., Pal, A., Burgess, C., Glorot, X., Botvinick, M., Mohamed, S., and Lerchner, A. (2017). beta-VAE: Learning basic visual concepts with a constrained variational framework. In *Proc. of the 5th International Conference on Learning Representations (ICLR)*, Toulon, France. 18

Hinton, G., Vinyals, O., and Dean, J. (2015). Distilling the knowledge in a neural network. In *NIPS Deep Learning Workshop*, Montreal, Canada. 18

Hoeffding, W. (1952). The large-sample power of tests based on permutations of observations. *Annals of Mathematical Statistics*, 23:169–192. DOI: 10.1214/aoms/1177729436 101, 113

Hutter, F., Hoss, H., and Leyton-Brown, K. (2014). An efficient approach for assessing hyperparameter importance. In *Proc. of the 31st International Conference on Machine Learning (ICML)*, Beijing, China. 75, 87, 88

Inhelder, B. and Piaget, J. (1958). *The Growth of Logical Thinking from Childhood to Adolescence*. Basic Books. DOI: 10.1037/10034-000 4, 13

Jia, R. and Liang, P. (2017). Adversarial examples for evaluating reading comprehension systems. In *Proc. of the Conference on Empirical Methods in Natural Language Processing (EMNLP)*, Copenhagen, Denmark. DOI: 10.18653/v1/d17-1215 9, 10

Jiang, Y., Neyshabur, B., Mobahi, H., Krishnan, D., and Bengio, S. (2019). Fantastic generalization measures and where to find them. In *International Conference on Learning Representations (ICLR)*, Addis Ababa, Ethiopia. 79

Jiang, Z. (2018). Using the linear mixed-effect model framework to estimate generalizability variance components in R. *Methodology*, 14(3):133–142. DOI: 10.1027/1614-2241/a000149 68, 71, 83

Jones, K. S. (1972). A statistical interpretation of term specificity and its application in retrieval. *Journal of Documentation*, 28:11–21. DOI: 10.7551/mitpress/12274.003.0037 33, 41

Karimova, S., Simianer, P., and Riezler, S. (2018). A user-study on online adaptation of neural machine translation to human post-edits. *Machine Translation*, 32(4):309–324. DOI: 10.1007/s10590-018-9224-8 66

Kaufmann, S., Rosset, S., and Perlich, C. (2011). Leakage in data mining: Formulation, detection, and avoidance. In *Proc. of the Conference on Knowledge Discovery and Data Mining (KDD)*, San Diego, CA. DOI: 10.1145/2020408.2020496 2, 10, 26, 45

Kawaguchi, K., Kaelbling, L. P., and Bengio, Y. (2020). Generalization in deep learning. *CoRR*. 2

Kim, B., Kim, H., Kim, K., Kim, S., and Kim, J. (2019). Learning not to learn: Training deep neural networks with biased data. In *Proc. of the IEEE/CVF Conference on Computer Vision and Pattern Recognition (CVPR)*, Long Beach, CA. DOI: 10.1109/cvpr.2019.00922 10, 25

Kim, Y. (2014). Convolutional neural networks for sentence classification. In *Proc. of the Conference on Empirical Methods in Natural Language Processing (EMNLP)*, Doha, Qatar. DOI: 10.3115/v1/d14-1181 18

Kim, Y. and Rush, A. M. (2016). Sequence-level knowledge distillation. In *Proc. of the Conference on Empirical Methods in Natural Language Processing (EMNLP)*, Austin, TX. DOI: 10.18653/v1/d16-1139 18

Koehn, P. (2004). Statistical significance tests for machine translation evaluation. In *Proc. of the Conference on Empirical Methods in Natural Language Processing (EMNLP)*, Barcelona, Spain. 91

Koo, T. K. and Li, M. Y. (2016). A guideline of selecting and reporting intraclass correlations coefficients for reliability research. *Journal of Chiropractic Medicine*, 15:155–163. DOI: 10.1016/j.jcm.2016.02.012 71, 74, 81, 83

Korb, K. (2004). Introduction: Machine learning as philosophy of science. *Minds and Machines*, 14(4):1–7. DOI: 10.1023/b:mind.0000045986.90956.7f 1

Krantz, D. H., Luce, R. D., Suppes, P., and Tversky, A. (1971). *Foundations of Measurement*. Academic Press. DOI: 10.2307/3172791 15

Kreutzer, J., Berger, N., and Riezler, S. (2020). Correct me if you can: Learning from error corrections and markings. In *Proc. of the 22nd Annual Conference of the European Association for Machine Translation (EAMT)*, Lisbon, Portugal. 66, 71, 72, 81, 82, 83, 84, 85, 92, 104, 106, 107, 111, 114

Krippendorff, K. (2004). *Content Analysis. An Introduction to its Methodology*. Sage. DOI: 10.1111/j.1468-4446.2007.00153_10.x 55, 56, 57, 58, 61, 88

Kuwa, T., Schamoni, S., and Riezler, S. (2020). Embedding meta-textual information for improved learning to rank. In *The 28th International Conference on Computational Linguistics (COLING)*. DOI: 10.18653/v1/2020.coling-main.487 11, 33

Lapuschkin, S., Wäldchen, S., Binder, A., Montavon, G., Samek, W., and Müller, K. (2019). Unmasking clever hans predictors and assessing what machines really learn. *Nature Communications*, 10(1):1–8. DOI: 10.1038/s41467-019-08987-4 17

Larsen, R. J. and Marx, M. L. (2012). *Mathematical Statistics and its Applications*, 5th ed., Prentice Hall. 20, 91, 93, 94, 101, 102, 108, 113

Lin, C.-Y. and Hovy, E. (2003). Automatic evaluation of summaries using n-gram co-occurrence statistics. In *Proc. of the Human Language Technology Conference of the North American Chapter of the Association for Computational Linguistics (HLT-NAACL)*, Edmonton, Canada. DOI: 10.3115/1073445.1073465 65

Locatello, F., Bauer, S., Lucic, M., Raetsch, G., Gelly, S., Schölkopf, B., and Bachem, O. (2019). Challenging common assumptions in the unsupervised learning of disentangled representations. In *Proc. of the 36th International Conference on Machine Learning (ICML)*, Long Beach, CA. 18

Lones, M. A. (2021). How to avoid machine learning pitfalls: A guide for academic researchers. *CoRR*. 2

Lord, F. M. and Novick, M. R. (1968). *Statistical Theories of Mental Test Scores*. Addison-Wesley. 12, 66, 87

Lou, Y., Caruana, R., and Gehrke, J. (2012). Intelligible models for classification and regression. In *Proc. of the 18th ACM SIGKDD International Conference on Knowledge Discovery and Data Mining*, London, UK. DOI: 10.1145/2339530.2339556 115

Lucic, M., Kurach, K., Michalski, M., Bousquet, O., and Gelly, S. (2018). Are GANs created equal? A large-scale study. In *Proc. of the 32nd International Conference on Neural Information Processing Systems (NIPS)*, Montréal, Canada. 2, 62, 63, 64, 65, 75, 92

Luong, T., Pham, H., and Manning, C. D. (2015). Effective approaches to attention-based neural machine translation. In *EMNLP*, Lisbon, Portugal. DOI: 10.18653/v1/d15-1166 82

Magdy, W. and Jones, G. J. F. (2010). Applying the KISS principle for the CLEF- IP 2010 prior art candidate patent search task. In *Proc. of the CLEF Workshop*, Padua, Italy. 4, 11, 17, 41

Mahdabi, P. and Crestani, F. (2014). Query-driven mining of citation networks for patent citation retrieval and recommendation. In *Proc. of the 23rd ACM International Conference on Information and Knowledge Management (CIKM)*, Shanghai, China. DOI: 10.1145/2661829.2661899 11

Manning, C. D., Raghavan, P., and Schütze, H. (2008). *Introduction to Information Retrieval*. Cambridge University Press. DOI: 10.1017/cbo9780511809071 43, 47, 65

Marie, B., Fujita, A., and Rubino, R. (2021). Scientific credibility of machine translation research: A meta-evaluation of 769 papers. In *Proc. of the 59th Annual Meeting of the Association for Computational Linguistics and the 11th International Joint Conference on Natural Language Processing (ACL-IJCNLP)*. DOI: 10.18653/v1/2021.acl-long.566 91

Markus, K. A. and Borsboom, D. (2013). *Frontiers of Test Validity Theory. Measurement, Causation, and Meaning*. Routledge. DOI: 10.4324/9780203501207 14

McCoy, T., Pavlick, E., and Linzen, T. (2019). Right for the wrong reasons: Diagnosing syntactic heuristics in natural language inference. In *Proc. of the 57th Annual Meeting of the Association for Computational Linguistics (ACL)*, Florence, Italy. DOI: 10.18653/v1/p19-1334 9, 10, 21, 25

McCullagh, P. and Nelder, J. (1989). *Generalized Linear Models*, 2nd ed., Chapman and Hall. DOI: 10.1201/9780203753736 29

McCulloch, C. E. and Searle, S. R. (2001). *Generalized, Linear, and Mixed Models*. Wiley. DOI: 10.1002/0471722073 66, 68, 125

McGraw, K. O. and Wong, S. P. (1996). Forming inferences about some intraclass correlation coefficients. *Psychological Methods*, 1(1):30–46. DOI: 10.1037/1082-989x.1.1.30 68

McShane, B. B., Gal, D., Gelman, A., Robert, C., and Tackett, J. L. (2019). Abandon statistical significance. *The American Statistician*, 73(sup1):235–245. DOI: 10.1080/00031305.2018.1527253 98, 100, 104

Mead, R., Gilmour, S., and Mead, A. (2012). *Statistical Principles for the Design of Experiments*. Cambridge University Press. DOI: 10.1017/cbo9781139020879 1

Michell, J. (2004). *Measurement on Psychology*. Cambridge University Press. DOI: 10.1017/cbo9780511490040 15

Mikolov, T., tau Yih, W., and Zweig, G. (2013). Linguistic regularities in continuous space word representations. In *Proc. of the Conference of the North American Chapter of the Association for Computational Linguistics: Human Language Technologies (NAACL-HLT)*, Atlanta, GA. 18

Miller, T. (2017). Explanation in artificial intelligence: Insights from the social sciences. *CoRR*. DOI: 10.1016/j.artint.2018.07.007 17

Mitchell, T., Cohen, W., Hruschka, E., Talukdar, P., Yang, B., Betteridge, J., Carlson, A., Dalvi, B., Gardner, M., Kisiel, B., Krishnamurthy, J., Lao, N., Mazaitis, K., Mohamed, T., Nakashole, N., Platanios, E., Ritter, A., Samadi, M., Settles, B., Wang, R., Wijaya, D., Gupta, A., Chen, X., Saparov, A., Greaves, M., and Welling, J. (2015). Never-ending learning. In *Proc. of the 29th Conference on Artificial Intelligence (AAAI)*, Austin, TX. DOI: 10.1145/3191513 25

140 BIBLIOGRAPHY

Nadeau, C. and Bengio, Y. (1999). Inference for the generalization error. In *Advances in Neural Information Processing Systems (NIPS)*, Denver, CO. 65, 92

Narens, L. (1985). *Abstract Measurement Theory*. Cambridge University Press. 15

Nemati, S., Holder, A., Razmi, F., Stanley, M. D., Clifford, G. D., and Buchman, T. G. (2018). An interpretable machine learning model for accurate prediction of sepsis in the ICU. *Critical Care Medicine*, 46(4):547–553. DOI: 10.1097/ccm.0000000000002936 11

Neyman, J. and Pearson, E. S. (1933). On the problem of the most efficient tests of statistical hypotheses. *Philosophical Transactions of the Royal Society of London. Series A*, 231:289–337. DOI: 10.1098/rsta.1933.0009 5, 92, 101, 102, 113

Nie, Y., Williams, A., Dinan, E., Bansal, M., Weston, J., and Kiela, D. (2020). Adversarial NLI: A new benchmark for natural language understanding. In *Proc. of the 58th Annual Meeting of the Association for Computational Linguistics (ACL)*. DOI: 10.18653/v1/2020.acl-main.441 21, 25

Niven, T. and Kao, H.-Y. (2019). Probing neural network comprehension of natural language arguments. In *Proc. of the 57th Annual Meeting of the Association for Computational Linguistics (ACL)*, Florence, Italy. DOI: 10.18653/v1/p19-1459 9

Noreen, E. W. (1989). *Computer Intensive Methods for Testing Hypotheses. An Introduction*. Wiley. 97, 100, 101

Papineni, K., Roukos, S., Ward, T., and Zhu, W.-J. (2002). Bleu: A method for automatic evaluation of machine translation. In *Proc. of the 40th Annual Meeting on Association for Computational Linguistics (ACL)*, Philadelphia, PA. DOI: 10.3115/1073083.1073135 57, 65, 91, 96, 100

Passonneau, R. J. and Carpenter, B. (2014). The benefits of a model of annotation. *Transactions of the Association for Computational Linguistics (TACL)*, 2:311–326. DOI: 10.1162/tacl_a_00185 87

Paun, S., Carpenter, B., Chamberlain, J., Hovy, D., Kruschwitz, U., and Poesio, M. (2018). Comparing Bayesian models of annotation. In *Transactions of the Association for Computational Linguistics (TACL)*, 6:571–585. DOI: 10.1162/tacl_a_00040 87

Pawitan, Y. (2001). *In All Likelihood. Statistical Modelling and Inference Using Likelihood*. Clarendon Press. 5, 128

Pearl, J. (2009). *Causality: Models, Reasoning, and Inference*, 2nd ed., Cambridge University Press. DOI: 10.1017/cbo9780511803161 20

Peters, J., Bühlmann, P., and Meinshausen, N. (2016). Causal inference using invariant prediction: Identification and confidence intervals. *Journal of the Royal Statistical Society, Series B*, 78(5):947–1012. 20, 25

Peters, J., Janzing, D., and Schölkopf, B. (2017). *Elements of Causal Inference: Foundations and Learning Algorithms*. MIT Press. 20

Pinheiro, J. C. and Bates, D. M. (2000). *Mixed-Effects Models in S and S-PLUS*. Springer. DOI: 10.1007/978-1-4419-0318-1 5, 68, 89, 92, 106, 112, 125

Piroi, F. and Tait, J. (2010). CLEF-IP 2010: Retrieval experiments in the intellectual property domain. In *Proc. of the Conference on Multilingual and Multimodal Information Access Evaluation (CLEF)*, Padua, Italy. 4, 11, 32, 50

Plesser, H. E. (2018). Reproducability vs. replicability: A brief history of a confused terminology. *Frontiers in Neuroinformatics*, 11(76):1–4. DOI: 10.3389/fninf.2017.00076 56

Poliak, A., Naradowsky, J., Haldar, A., Rudinger, R., and Van Durme, B. (2018). Hypothesis only baselines in natural language inference. In *Proc. of the 7th Joint Conference on Lexical and Computational Semantics*, New Orleans, LA. DOI: 10.18653/v1/s18-2023 9, 10

Qin, T., Liu, T.-Y., Xu, J., and Li, H. (2010). LETOR: A benchmark collection for research on learning to rank for information retrieval. *Information Retrieval Journal*, 13(4):346–374. DOI: 10.1007/s10791-009-9123-y 32

Rei, R., Stewart, C., Farinha, A. C., and Lavie, A. (2020). COMET: A neural framework for MT evaluation. In *Proc. of the Conference on Empirical Methods in Natural Language Processing (EMNLP)*. DOI: 10.18653/v1/2020.emnlp-main.213 88

Reyna, M. A., Josef, C. S., Jeter, R., Shashikumar, S. P., Westover, M. B., Nemati, S., Clifford, G. D., and Sharma, A. (2019). Early prediction of sepsis from clinical data: The physionet/computing in cardiology challenge 2019. *Critical Care Medicine*, 48(2):210–217. DOI: 10.1097/CCM.0000000000004145 11, 36, 50

Ribeiro, M. T., Singh, S., and Guestrin, C. (2016). Why should I trust you? Explaining the predictions of any classifier. In *Proc. of the Conference on Knowledge Discovery and Data Mining (KDD)*, San Francisco, CA. DOI: 10.1145/2939672.2939778 17

Riezler, S. and Maxwell, J. (2005). On some pitfalls in automatic evaluation and significance testing for MT. In *Proc. of the ACL Workshop on Intrinsic and Extrinsic Evaluation Measures for MT and/or Summarization*, Ann Arbor, MI. 91, 101

Robertson, S. and Zaragoza, H. (2009). The probabilistic relevance framework: BM25 and beyond. *Foundations and Trends in Information Retrieval*, 3(4):333–389. DOI: 10.1561/1500000019 32

Robertson, S. E. and Kanoulas, E. (2012). On per-topic variance in IR evaluation. In *Proc. of the 35th International ACM SIGIR Conference on Research and Development in Information Retrieval*, Portland, OR. DOI: 10.1145/2348283.2348402 87, 112

Rosenfeld, E., Ravikumar, P., and Risteski, A. (2021). The risks of invariant risk minimization. In *Proc. of the International Conference on Learning Representations (ICLR)*. 20

Rosset, S., Perlich, C., Swirszcz, G., Melville, P., and Liu, Y. (2009). Medical data mining: Insights from winning two competitions. *Data Mining and Knowledge Discovery*, 20:439–468. DOI: 10.1007/s10618-009-0158-x 10, 17, 26, 27

Rudd, K. E., Johnson, S. C., Agesa, K. M., Shackelford, K. A., Tsoi, D., Kievlan, D. R., Colombara, D. V., Ikuta, K. S., Kissoon, N., Finfer, S., Fleischmann-Struzek, C., Machado, F. R., Reinhart, K. K., Rowan, K., Seymour, C. W., Watson, R. S., West, T. E., Marinho, F., Hay, S. I., Lozano, R., Lopez, A. D., Angus, D. C., Murray, C. J. L., and Naghavi, M. (2020). Global, regional, and national sepsis incidence and mortality, 1990–2017: Analysis for the global burden of disease study. *The Lancet*, 395(10219):200–211. 12, 36

Rumelhart, D. E., Hinton, G. E., and Williams, R. J. (1986). Learning representations by back-propagating errors. *Nature*, 323:533–536. DOI: 10.1038/323533a0 76

Schamoni, S., Lindner, H. A., Schneider-Lindner, V., Thiel, M., and Riezler, S. (2019). Leveraging implicit expert knowledge for non-circular machine learning in sepsis prediction. *Journal of Artificial Intelligence in Medicine*, 100:1–9. DOI: 10.1016/j.artmed.2019.101725 2, 11, 17, 36, 47, 52, 76

Schamoni, S. and Riezler, S. (2015). Combining orthogonal information in large-scale cross-language information retrieval. In *Proc. of the 38th Annual ACM SIGIR Conference*, Santiago, Chile. DOI: 10.1145/2766462.2767805 11

Schlegel, V., Nenadic, G., and Batista-Navarro, R. (2020). Beyond leaderboards: A survey of methods for revealing weaknesses in natural language inference data and models. *CoRR*. 10, 21

Schölkopf, B. (2019). Causality for machine learning. *CoRR*. 1

Schölkopf, B., Locatello, F., Bauer, S., Ke, N. R., Kalchbrenner, N., Goyal, A., and Bengio, Y. (2021). Toward causal representation learning. *Proc. of the IEEE*, 109(5):612–634. DOI: 10.1109/jproc.2021.3058954 20

Scott, W. A. (1955). Reliability of content analysis: The case of nominal scale coding. *Public Opinion Quarterly*, 19:321–325. DOI: 10.1086/266577 57

Searle, S. R., Casella, G., and McCulloch, C. E. (1992). *Variance Components*. Wiley. 5, 66, 79, 80

Sellam, T., Yadlowsky, S., Wei, J., Saphra, N., D'Amour, A., Linzen, T., Bastings, J., Turc, I., Eisenstein, J., Das, D., Tenney, I., and Pavlick, E. (2021). The multiberts: BERT reproductions for robustness analysis. *CoRR*. 99, 113

Seymour, C. W., Liu, V. X., Iwashyna, T. J., Brunkhorst, F. M., Rea, T. D., Scherag, A., Rubenfeld, G., Kahn, J. M., Shankar-Hari, M., Singer, M., Deutschman, C. S., Escobar, G. J., and Angus, D. C. (2016). Assessment of clinical criteria for sepsis for the third international consensus definitions for sepsis and septic shock (Sepsis-3). *JAMA*, 315(8):762–774. DOI: 10.1001/jama.2016.0288 11, 36

Shao, J. (2003). *Mathematical Statistics*, 2nd ed., Springer. DOI: 10.1007/b97553 62

Shen, Z., Liu, J., He, Y., Zhang, X., Xu, R., Yu, H., and Cui, P. (2021). Towards out-of-distribution generalization: A survey. *CoRR*. 2

Shoukri, M. M. (2011). *Measures of Interobserver Agreement and Reliability*, 2nd ed., Taylor and Francis. DOI: 10.1201/b10433 55

Shrout, P. E. and Fleiss, J. L. (1979). Intraclass correlations: Uses in assessing rater reliability. *Psychological Bulletin*, 86(2):420–428. DOI: 10.1037/0033-2909.86.2.420 68

Simianer, P., Karimova, S., and Riezler, S. (2016). A post-editing interface for immediate adaptation in statistical machine translation. In *Proc. of the Conference on Computational Linguistics: System Demonstrations (COLING Demos)*, Osaka, Japan. 66

Singer, M., Deutschman, C. S., and Seymour, C. W. (2016). The third international consensus definitions for sepsis and septic shock (Sepsis-3). *JAMA*, 315(8):801–810. DOI: 10.1001/jama.2016.0287 11, 36

Sneed, J. D. (1971). *The Logical Structure of Mathematical Physics*. D. Reidel. DOI: 10.1007/978-94-010-3066-3 16

Snover, M., Dorr, B., Schwartz, R., Micciulla, L., and Makhoul, J. (2006). A study of translation edit rate with targeted human annotation. In *Proc. of the 7th Conference of the Association for Machine Translation in the Americas (AMTA)*, Cambridge, MA. 57, 66, 82, 96, 100

Søgaard, A., Ebert, S., Bastings, J., and Filippova, K. (2021). We need to talk about random splits. In *Proc. of the 16th Conference of the European Chapter of the Association for Computational Linguistics (EACL)*. DOI: 10.18653/v1/2021.eacl-main.156 12, 114

Srivastava, N., Hinton, G., Krizhevsky, A., Sutskever, I., and Salakhutdinov, R. (2014). Dropout: A simple way to prevent neural networks from overfitting. *Journal of Machine Learning Research*, 15(56):1929–1958. 76

Stegmüller, W. (1979). *The Structuralist View of Theories. A Possible Analogue of the Bourbaki Programme in Physical Science.* Springer. DOI: 10.1007/978-3-642-95360-6 16

Stegmüller, W. (1986). *Probleme und Resultate der Wissenschaftstheorie und Analytischen Philosophie. Band II: Theorie und Erfahrung. Zweiter Teilband: Therienstrukturen und Theoriendynamik,* 2nd ed., Springer. 16

Stevens, S. S. (1946). On the theory of scales of measurement. *Science*, 103(2684):677–680. DOI: 10.1126/science.103.2684.677 14, 15, 17, 25

Strubell, E., Ganesh, A., and McCallum, A. (2019). Energy and policy considerations for deep learning in NLP. In *Proc. of the 57th Annual Meeting of the Association for Computational Linguistics (ACL)*, Florence, Italy. DOI: 10.18653/v1/p19-1355 75

Student, W. S. G. (1908). The probable error of a mean. *Biometrika*, 6(1):1–25. DOI: 10.2307/2331554 91

Tan, S., Caruana, R., Hooker, G., and Lou, Y. (2018). Distill-and-compare: Auditing black-box models using transparent model distillation. In *Proc. of AIES*, New Orleans, LA. DOI: 10.1145/3278721.3278725 18

Tang, R., Lee, J., Xin, J., Liu, X., Yu, Y., and Lin, J. (2020). Showing your work doesn't always work. In *Proc. of the 58th Annual Meeting of the Association for Computational Linguistics (ACL)*. DOI: 10.18653/v1/2020.acl-main.246 63, 75

Tomaschek, F., Hendrix, P., and Baayen, R. H. (2018). Strategies for addressing collinearity in multivariate linguistic data. *Journal of Phonetics*, 71:249–267. DOI: 10.1016/j.wocn.2018.09.004 17

van der Vaart, A. W. (1998). *Asymptotic Statistics.* Cambridge University Press. DOI: 10.1017/cbo9780511802256 93, 101, 103, 128

Vapnik, V. N. (1998). *Statistical Learning Theory.* Wiley. 1

Vincent, J., Moreno, R., Takala, J., Willatts, S., Mendonça, A. D., Bruining, H., Reinhart, C., Suter, P., and Thijs, L. (1996). The SOFA (Sepsis-related Organ Failure Assessment) score to describe organ dysfunction/failure. *Intensive Care Medicine*, 22(7):707–710. DOI: 10.1007/bf01709751 11, 36

von Luxburg, U. and Schölkopf, B. (2011). Statistical learning theory: Models, concepts, and results. In Gabbay, D., Hartmann, S., and Woods, J., Eds., *Handbook of the History of Logic: Inductive Logic*, 10:651–706, Elsevier. DOI: 10.1016/b978-0-444-52936-7.50016-1 1

Voorhees, E. M., Samarov, D., and Soboroff, I. (2017). Using replicates in information retrieval evaluation. *ACM Transactions on Information Systems*, 36(2):1–31. DOI: 10.1145/3086701 87

Webb, N. M., Shavelson, R. J., and Haertel, E. H. (2006). Reliability coefficients and generalizability theory. *Handbook of Statistics*, 26:81–214. DOI: 10.1016/s0169-7161(06)26004-8 87

West, B. T., Welch, K. B., and Galecki, A. T. (2007). *Linear Mixed Models: A Practical Guide Using Statistical Software*. Chapman & Hall/CRC. DOI: 10.1201/9781420010435 68, 125

Wilks, S. S. (1938). The large-sample distribution of the likelihood ratio for testing composite hypotheses. *Annals of Mathematical Statistics*, 19:60–92. DOI: 10.1214/aoms/1177732360 103, 113, 127

Williams, A., Nangia, N., and Bowman, S. (2018). A broad-coverage challenge corpus for sentence understanding through inference. In *Proc. of the Conference of the North American Chapter of the Association for Computational Linguistics: Human Language Technologies (NAACL:HLT)*, New Orleans, LA. DOI: 10.18653/v1/n18-1101 21

Wood, S. N. (2003). Thin plate regression splines. *Journal of the Royal Statistical Society, Series B*, 65(1):95–114. DOI: 10.1111/1467-9868.00374 119

Wood, S. N. (2011). Fast stable restricted maximum likelihood and marginal likelihood estimation of semiparametric generalized linear models. *Journal of the Royal Statistical Society, Series B (Statistical Methodology)*, 73(1):3–36. DOI: 10.1111/j.1467-9868.2010.00749.x 112

Wood, S. N. (2017). *Generalized Additive Models. An Introduction with R*, 2nd ed., Chapman & Hall/CRC. DOI: 10.1201/9781315370279 xv, 3, 30, 31, 68, 86, 115, 119, 125

Wood, S. N., Pya, N., and Säfken, B. (2016). Smoothing parameter and model selection for general smooth models. *Journal of the American Statistical Association*, 111(516):1548–1575. DOI: 10.1080/01621459.2016.1180986 119

Yeh, A. (2000). More accurate tests for the statistical significance of result differences. In *Proc. of the 18th International Conference on Computational Linguistics (COLING)*, Saarbrücken. DOI: 10.3115/992730.992783 91, 96

Zhai, C. and Lafferty, J. (2001). A study of smoothing methods for language models applied to information retrieval. In *Proc. of the 24th Annual International Conference on Research and Development in Information Retrieval (SIGIR)*, New York. DOI: 10.1145/383952.384019 33

Zhang, T., Kishore, V., Wu, F., Weinberger, K. Q., and Artzi, Y. (2020). BERTScore: Evaluating text generation with BERT. In *International Conference on Learning Representations (ICLR)*. 88

Zhao, X., Liu, J. S., and Deng, K. (2013). Assumptions behind intercoder reliability indices. *Communication Yearbook*, 36:419–480. DOI: 10.1080/23808985.2013.11679142 61

146   BIBLIOGRAPHY

Zimmer, L., Lindauer, M., and Hutter, F. (2020). Auto-pytorch tabular: Multi-fidelity metalearning for efficient and robust autodl. *CoRR*. 75, 77, 87, 88

Authors' Biographies

STEFAN RIEZLER

Stefan Riezler is a full professor in the Department of Computational Linguistics at Heidelberg University, Germany since 2010, and also co-opted in Informatics at the Department of Mathematics and Computer Science. He received his Ph.D. (with distinction) in Computational Linguistics from the University of Tübingen in 1998, conducted post-doctoral work at Brown University in 1999, and spent a decade in industry research (Xerox PARC, Google Research). His research focus is on interactive machine learning for natural language processing problems especially for the application areas of cross-lingual information retrieval and statistical machine translation. He is engaged as an editorial board member of the main journals of the field—*Computational Linguistics* and *Transactions of the Association for Computational Linguistics*—and is a regular member of the program committee of various natural language processing and machine learning conferences. He has published more than 100 journal and conference papers in these areas. He also conducts interdisciplinary research as member of the Interdisciplinary Center for Scientific Computing (IWR), for example, on the topic of early prediction of sepsis using machine learning and natural language processing techniques.

MICHAEL HAGMANN

Michael Hagmann is a graduate research assistant in the Department of Computational Linguistics at Heidelberg University, Germany, since 2019. He holds an M.Sc. in Statistics (with distinction) from the University of Vienna, Austria. He received an award for the best Master's thesis in Applied Statistics from the Austrian Statistical Society. He has worked as a medical statistician at the medical faculty of Heidelberg University in Mannheim, Germany and in the section for Medical Statistics at the Medical University of Vienna, Austria. His research focus is on statistical methods for data science and, recently, NLP. He has published more than 50 papers in journals for medical research and mathematical statistics.

Printed in the United States
by Baker & Taylor Publisher Services